A Marian Prayer Book

*A Treasury of Prayers, Hymns,
and Meditations*

Edited by
Pamela Moran

HarperCollins*Religious*
An Imprint of HarperCollins*Publishers*

HarperCollins*Religious*
Part of HarperCollins*Publishers*
77-85 Fulham Palace Road, London, W6 8JB

First published in the USA in 1991 by Servant Publications,
and in Great Britain in 1992 by HarperCollins*Religious*.

10 9 8 7 6 5 4 3 2 1

A catalogue record for this book is available from the British Library.

ISBN 0 00 599344-X

Printed with ecclesiastical approval.
Nothing Contrary to Faith: Reverend James A. Murray Censor Liborum
Approved: † Most Reverend Kenneth Povish
                    Bishop of the Diocese of Lansing
                    Given at the Chancery Office, Diocese of Lansing, July 7, 1991
This approval is an official declaration that a book or pamphlet is free from
doctrinal or moral error. No implication is contained therein that those who
have given this approval agree with the contents, opinions, or statements
expressed.

Scripture texts in this work are taken from the Revised Standard Version of
the Bible, copyright © 1946, 1952, and 1971, by the Division of Christian
Education of the National Council of Churches in the U.S.A., and are used by
permission.

Cover design by Michael Andaloro
Cover art courtesy: Scala/Art Resource, NY

Printed and bound in the United States of America

A MARIAN PRAYER BOOK

Dedicated to Mary, my spiritual mother,
that she may use this book
to draw her children closer to God,
and to my mother, Elizabeth,
who has been such an example
of the faithful love of a
wife and mother.

Mary, Mother of God,
we are the poor soil
and the dry dust;
we are hard with a cold frost.

Be warmth to the world;
be the thaw,
warm on the cold frost;
be the thaw that melts,
that the tender shoot of Christ,
piercing the hard heart,
flower to a spring in us.

Be hands that are rocking the world
to a kind rhythm of love;
that the incoherence of war
and the chaos of our unrest
be soothed to a lullaby;
and the round and sorrowful world,
in your hands,
the cradle of God.   **"The Reed"**
                       by Caryll Houselander

Contents

Introduction

GOD MUST HAVE a wonderful sense of humor. I can almost hear him chuckling now as he watches me laboring to finish this book about Mary. You see, I was born in Georgia and raised as a Southern Baptist. Mary was not part of my culture at all—if anything she was held in suspicion, along with anything Catholic. But God is full of surprises and blessings which far exceed our wildest dreams.

My spiritual journey has been long and rich, from water baptism by full immersion at age seventeen in front of a Baptist congregation, through fundamentalism study at a Bible college, through the charismatic renewal, through years of a fruitless search for the "perfect denomination," and finally to the Catholic church.

After months of intense soul-searching, I entered the Catholic church about seventeen years ago, three days before I married my cradle-Catholic husband. My questions were far from answered—at least to my intellectual satisfaction—but I believed God made it clear to me that he wanted me to become a Catholic. And so I joyfully obeyed, without knowing how it would all work out. I have never been sorry about my decision. My spiritual journey within Catholicism has been long and rich as well. But I can now honestly say that I feel very much at home.

GETTING TO KNOW MARY

During the last few years, my husband, Bill, has experienced a profound renewal in his relationship with Mary, the mother of Jesus. A negative reaction to certain aspects of Marian devotion had resulted in his shutting out Mary for years, but God unexpectedly broke through these barriers. Perhaps through Bill's and Mary's intercession, I myself began to experience this same grace of coming to know the love of my spiritual mother.

Mary is such a lady that she doesn't push her way into someone's life, but waits to be invited. John Lynch calls her "a woman wrapped in silence." Perhaps it was actually easier for me to get to know Mary since I didn't have to deal with a lot of "cultural baggage" from the past. I had no preconceived notions to overcome. The reality of a spiritual mother was all new to me, fresh with wonder and awe at the gracious gift of God.

An African word for mother translates "she who hears when I call." That has been my experience of Mary. Whenever I call, she hears and graciously answers. Her gentle goodness is like a soft and waiting lap when I'm sad or lonely, or when the little girl in me needs hugs and kisses. And yet she is full of strength, ever zealous to call me on to love and serve God.

I can honestly say that my spiritual life has been profoundly changed over the last several months as a result of working on this book. In the early stages of my research, I often called out to Mary in desperation because of the overwhelming task which faced me. For months I felt as if I were swimming in the deepest ocean, with no land in sight. Sometimes I feared I would sink beneath the waves and drown. Now that land is in sight, I have gratefully thanked Mary for her intercession and help, and asked her to use this book to further the kingdom of God.

One winter day when I was reading about how the saints experienced Our Lady's presence, I was inspired to ask Mary to show herself to me in some tangible way. So I asked her for a favor: if she were really there and listening to me (I was not totally convinced at that point), to please have the nine-year-old girl next door invite my seven-year-old daughter over to go sledding in their yard after school.

Besides providing some outdoor fun, I must admit my motives were somewhat selfish: having my daughter gone would provide me with more precious time to work on this book! I figured Mary had some investment in that herself. But because of their age difference, such an invitation was also a rare occurrence. I believed this would give Mary an opportunity to show herself.

Just a few minutes after my daughter arrived home from school, she told me the neighbor girl had just asked her on the bus if she could come over and go sledding that afternoon! I was amazed—and very grateful. That was just one small example of Mary's gracious response to our needs. From then on, I felt Mary's presence more consistently—as if she were looking over my shoulder as I worked.

I have since regularly taken much larger needs to Mary, confident of leaving them in her hands. In fact, I tend to give Mary my most persistent and seemingly insoluble problems. Although the answers to those might not come so quickly, I trust these problems will be resolved eventually, through Mary's intercession.

THE PURPOSE OF THIS BOOK

Why did I embark on this project? Actually, because my publisher needed an editor for this book and asked me if I wanted the job. My husband and I both argued that my Protestant background left me at a serious disadvantage, but our protests were to no avail. And so I began. (My deepest thanks to Servant Publications for their confidence in me and for allowing me this unexpected opportunity. My special thanks to my editor, Dave Came, who has offered expert guidance and answered my many questions with great patience.)

Besides working on what I knew to be a worthwhile project, my basic motivation was somewhat selfish: researching material on Mary would help *me* to learn more about the mother of Jesus. My knowledge in the area was actually very limited. I am even now far from an expert on Marian literature. But now that I have come to know more about Mary— and indeed come to know Mary personally—I want to share that immense good news with others.

My purpose in the pages that follow is that you yourself might get to know Mary better as your spiritual mother, to know the rich love and mercy available to us through this priceless gift of God.

I would be doing Mary a great injustice if this book were primarily intended to bring her honor and glory—for Mary herself in utmost humility returned all glory and honor to God. She knew without a doubt that all that she had was only a gift by the grace of God. And so ultimately, I wish to glorify God in these pages, that you may be drawn nearer to the source of life himself, through the intercession of Mary.

Mary is part of God's plan. God chose Mary to give us Jesus. The Father has chosen to heap honor upon the mother of his Son, just as he wishes to honor all of his servants. Mary serves as the model disciple: the one who loved God with all of her heart, all of her mind, and all of her soul. Her response to God was always yes. Mary wants to teach us how to surrender humbly all that we have and do to God, who loves us with such mercy and compassion.

As evidenced by a recent resurgence of devotion to Mary, the Holy Spirit is leading the church toward a better understanding of Mary as our mother. Mary's spiritual motherhood is constantly active. A mother never ceases to be a mother, never forgets her children. Mary is *still working* so that Jesus can be born in the hearts of all people. Her heart's desire is that all men and women would come to know the fullness of the love of God—most graphically demonstrated in the sacrifice of her Son Jesus on the cross.

Under the influence of the Holy Spirit, Mary welcomed Jesus in herself so that she could give him to the world. On the morning of Pentecost, Mary prayed along with those gathered in the upper room so that the Holy Spirit could blow powerfully into the lives of all of Jesus' disciples. On that day, Christ was born again in his body, which is the church.

God calls us to join with Mary's yes. In so doing, we welcome the grace and power of the Holy Spirit into our lives. Cardinal Suenens calls Mary "the short cut" to the Holy Spirit. The key to welcoming the outpouring of the Spirit is in uniting our faith with Mary's. We can pray with Mary as the disciples did in the upper room. By the power of the Holy Spirit, our prayer of faith can be translated into action. The good news is proclaimed. Men and women are spiritually reborn.

As we learn how to enter into a more dynamic relationship with Mary, we unloose the power of the Holy Spirit more fully in our own lives. In union with Mary, we participate in a more fruitful way in her mission to bring the light and life of Jesus to the ends of the earth. This prayer book is not meant to end in personal devotions, but to lead to practical evangelism and greater love of God and our neighbor.

HOW TO USE THIS PRAYER BOOK

Part One includes five chapters dealing with Mary as our mother, as the model disciple, as the model woman, as a mother who constantly prays for us, and as a messenger of God's love and mercy. To build your understanding of Mary, these five chapters are primarily composed of prayerful meditations and reflections on Mary by a wide variety of spiritual writers, thinkers, and saints.

Just a few of those quoted are Pope John Paul II, Cardinal Léon Joseph Suenens, Mother Teresa of Calcutta, George Montague, Basilea Schlink, Mother Angelica, St. Maximilian Kolbe, Edward Schillebeeckx, René Laurentin, Karl Rahner, Catherine de

Hueck Doherty, Bishop Fulton J. Sheen, Caryll Houselander, St. Francis de Sales, Cardinal John Henry Newman, Thomas Merton, St. Louis de Montfort, St. Alphonsus Liguori, and St. Bernard.

Each chapter is divided into several sections covering particular aspects which develop the main theme. For example, chapter one about Mary as our mother begins with the annunciation, the incarnation, the birth scene, and the care of Jesus—first as an infant and then as a growing boy. Having become more familiar with Mary as the mother of Jesus, we will then consider Mary as *our* spiritual mother who expresses her tender love and care for each of us in many personal and practical ways.

I found these readings to be very helpful in getting to know Mary as a very real human being who endured the same trials and difficulties that I often face as a mother. My own mother often told me, "You'll never know what it means to be a mother until you're a mother yourself." Now I know that she was right. The job of being a mother is tremendously demanding. It helps me a lot to know Mary is there to help me.

For example, one day this winter my daughter did not arrive home from school as usual. I kept looking out the window, but the school bus was nowhere in sight. Imagining the worst, I quickly began to panic. The bus was never late. After ten minutes, I drove to the school just a mile away, but no sign of her there.

Back home, I was again greeted by silence instead of my daughter's cheery smile.

Of course, I was praying all the while. I called a neighbor and learned that her son had not arrived home from school either. Because that morning had been a snow emergency, we guessed that perhaps the bus driver had driven the route in reverse order that day. That helped settle me down a little bit, but I was not really at peace until my daughter arrived home from school forty-five minutes later.

In the midst of my panic, I remembered Mary's experience of losing Jesus in Jerusalem—discussed in chapter four on Mary's role as an intercessor. Her motherly anxiety seemed very real to me. How could Mary possibly have gone through three whole days not knowing if Jesus were safe? I could barely last an hour! What a source of strength to know that I had a mother who understood my fears, and to be able to call on Mary's help and protection for my only child.

If you are new to Marian devotion, carefully read and pray through Part One as a way to explore the role Mary could have in your own life. Before you begin, be sure to ask God himself to reveal his mother to you as his special gift. You might want to read one section of a chapter each day. Each of these sections is fairly short and should not take more than ten minutes or so. Prayerfully meditating on these excerpts from a wide variety of writers will help you get to know Mary better.

I have opened each section with a poem or hymn relevant to the topic, and closed each one with a short prayer especially written for the theme of that chapter. After reading through each section, you could say the closing prayer as a simple way to call upon Mary.

You can use Part Two as a resource of prayers and devotions, or compose your own prayers if you keep a prayer journal. These prayers are just meant to be "starters" that help you speak to Mary in your own words. Chapter six offers more popular prayers from a variety of authors. Chapter seven contains a selection of more traditional prayers and Marian devotions, including a prayer especially written for each of the major Marian feast days.

Perhaps Marian devotion is already a strong part of your spirituality. You will probably enjoy reading through Part One in a meditative and prayerful way, to deepen and further your appreciation of Mary. Part Two can serve as a valuable resource of prayers for various occasions.

You may want to share this book with a friend who you think would benefit from getting to know more about Mary. This would be a fairly non-threatening way of sharing this precious gift of a mother with others. Mothers could use chapter three on womanhood as a help in forming their daughters in womanly character. Coming to know Mary as my mother and understanding her role in God's plan of redemption has been deeply healing and liberating for me as a woman.

While this book is ideal for personal use, it could also be a valuable resource for parish devotions or Marian groups. For example, parishes might use it for Marian prayer services and celebrations during the months of May and October and for Marian feast days. Parish libraries may want to keep several copies on hand as a prayer resource. You could bring it to the attention of your pastor or the director of religious education in your parish.

Marian apostolates or movements might use this book as a prayer resource for chapter meetings and as a nice gift for prospective members. Those making an individual retreat or group pilgrimage to the sites of Marian apparitions could take this book along as a prayer partner to help bring alive Mary's loving presence. Chapter five discusses Mary's role as a messenger of God's love and mercy, especially as she has manifested herself in Marian apparitions such as Fatima, Lourdes, and Guadalupe.

Whoever you are, my deepest prayer is that you may come to know the love and mercy of God expressed through Mary. I have found that heartfelt knowledge to be deeply transforming in my own life. I believe Mary has been uniquely blessed among humankind in knowing the love and mercy of God.

By the power of the Holy Spirit, God's grace so filled Mary that the Son of God himself took on human flesh within her womb.

If you don't yet know Mary, ask Jesus to introduce you to his mother. Mary wants you to know Jesus better, to know the love of God the Father more clearly, to experience more of the power of the Holy Spirit. Humbly open your heart to the love of God. Let Mary speak to you of God's immense love in the pages that follow. Listen to your mother—and you will never be the same again.

God, the almighty Father, willed that every generation sing the praise of Mary, the Mother of his Son. Let us glorify his name and ask of him: May Mary, full of grace, intercede for us!

Part One

Prayerful Meditations on Mary and Her Role

ONE

The Mother Jesus Gave Us

God wants us to experience the tender love of Mary our mother, just as we know his Fatherly love. The final gift Jesus gave us when he was dying on the cross was Mary, his own mother. As we retrace these awesome events of history, we begin to realize the magnitude and meaning of this precious gift. Our story begins when the Archangel Gabriel was sent from heaven to bring wonderful news: Mary was to bear God's Son.

The Annunciation

Was this His coming! I had hoped to see
A scene of wondrous glory, as was told
Of some great God who in a rain of gold

Broke open bars and fell on Danae;
Or a dread vision as when Semele,
Sickening for love and unappeased desire,
Prayed to see God's clear body, and the fire
Caught her brown limbs and slew her utterly.
With such glad dreams I sought this holy place,
And now with wondering eyes and heart I stand
Before this supreme mystery of Love:
Some kneeling girl with passionless pale face,
An angel with a lily in his hand,
And over both the white wings of a Dove.

"Ave Maria, Gratia Plena"
by Oscar Wilde

In the sixth month the angel Gabriel was sent from
God to a city of Galilee named Nazareth, to a virgin
betrothed to a man whose name was Joseph, of the
house of David; and the virgin's name was Mary.
And he came to her and said, "Hail, O favored one,
the Lord is with you!"

But she was greatly troubled at the saying, and
considered in her mind what sort of greeting this
might be. And the angel said to her, "Do not be
afraid, Mary, for you have found favor with God.
And behold, you will conceive in your womb and
bear a son, and you shall call his name Jesus...." And
Mary said to the angel, "How shall this be, since I
have no husband?"

And the angel said to her, "The Holy Spirit will
come upon you, and the power of the Most High will
overshadow you; therefore the child to be born will

be called holy, the Son of God. And behold, your kinswoman Elizabeth in her old age has also conceived a son; and this is the sixth month with her who was called barren. For with God nothing will be impossible." And Mary said, "Behold, I am the handmaid of the Lord; let it be to me according to your word." **Luke 1:26-38**

Many years ago an angel came to bring the good news to Mary. The Prince of Peace was anxious to come to earth and an angel was used to bring the good news that the Creator would become a little Child. The Prince of Peace was attracted to a young girl, who was a nobody in the eyes of the world. Even the angel could not understand why he was sent to a creature like that. But she was so beautiful that the King of Kings wanted to become flesh in her. She was so full of grace, so pure, so full of God.

She looked at the angel—she must have been surprised for she had never seen an angel—and asked, how? What are you saying? I don't understand what you are saying; it makes no sense to me. And the angel said simply that by the power of the Holy Spirit, Christ would be formed within her. And Mary answered simply: "Behold the handmaid of the Lord." **Mother Teresa of Calcutta**

Wisdom would become man provided that Mary consent. **St. Louis de Montfort**

How consistent it is with the incredible tenderness of God that His Christ, the Immortal Child, should be conceived by the power of the Spirit in the body of a child. That a child should bear a Child, to redeem the world.

Our Lady was at the most fourteen when the angel came to her; perhaps she was younger.

The whole world trembled on the word of a child, on a child's consent....

Our Lady said yes.

She said yes for us all.

It was as if the human race were a little dark house, without light or air, locked and latched.

The wind of the Spirit had beaten on the door, rattled the windows, tapped on the dark glass with the tiny hands of flowers, flung golden seed against it, even, in hours of storm, lashed it with the boughs of a great tree—the prophecy of the Cross—and yet the Spirit was outside. But one day a girl opened the door, and the little house was swept pure and sweet by the wind. Seas of light swept through it, and the light remained in it; and in that little house a Child was born and the Child was God. **Caryll Houselander**

But the Word was made flesh because a maiden of our race knelt down at the angel's message and in the freedom of her heart and with the total unconditional gift of herself said: Be it done unto me according to thy word. God willed this freely given love of his creature as the means by which the eternal Word of the Father should enter the world to take this world up into his own life. That was the way he willed to come into this world.   **Karl Rahner**

Behold the handmaid of the Lord; be it done unto me according to your word. What more beautiful, more humble, or more prudent answer could all the wisdom of men and angels together have invented, had they reflected for a million years? O powerful answer, which rejoiced Heaven and brought an immense sea of graces and blessings into the world!— answer which had scarcely fallen from the lips of Mary, before it drew the only-begotten Son of God from the bosom of His Eternal Father, to become Man in her most pure womb! Yes, indeed; for scarcely had she uttered these words when instantly *the Word was made flesh* (John 1:14): the Son of God became also the Son of Mary.   **St. Alphonsus**

> *Mary, help me to know more fully*
> *the precious gift of a mother.*
> *You always hear me when I call.*
> *Embrace me with your loving care*
> *and keep watch over my steps,*
> *that Jesus may be born in me.*
> *Through Christ our Lord. Amen.*

The Incarnation

A garden bower in flower
Grew waiting for God's hand:
Where no man ever trod,
This was the Gate of God.
The first bower was red—
Her lips which "welcome" said.
The second bower was blue—
Her eyes that let God through.
The third bower was white—
Her soul in God's sight.
Three bowers of love,
Now Christ from heaven above.

"God's Mother"
by Laurence Housman

Mary's yes shook and shaped all of history. At her con-sent, God came down from heaven to make the earth his home—not as a noble king, but as a tiny fetus begotten of the Holy Spirit within the womb of Mary. The story has become so familiar that we can easily miss the awesome reality that transpired—without a single trumpet blast, known only to a young Jewish girl in Nazareth.

The holy mystery of that moment is beyond the reach of human understanding, for no one has ever been granted such a mark of divine favor as Mary was when the Holy Spirit overshadowed her so that the Child Jesus would be formed within her as a human infant and she would give birth to the Holy One, the Son of God. A divine veil rests over this holy event.

We can only sense that streams of divine blessing must have come flowing down upon Mary in that hour when the Holy Spirit Himself, the Third Person of the Godhead, overshadowed her, perhaps moving over her as He once moved over the face of the waters when the earth was without form and void. Who can tell what happened to Mary when she came into such close contact with the Holiest of all—yes, when the Holy One, the Son of God, assumed human flesh within her! When Moses was honored with an encounter with God on Mount Sinai a radiance lay upon his features. What a divine radiance must have lain upon Mary, what a change must have come over her, when God Himself made His dwelling in her! **Basilea Schlink**

Therefore the Lord himself will give you a sign. Behold, a young woman shall conceive and bear a son, and shall call his name Immanuel. **Isaiah 7:14**

For nine months Christ grew in His Mother's body. By his own will she formed Him from herself, from the simplicity of her daily life.

She had nothing to give Him but herself.

He asked for nothing else.

She gave Him herself.

Working, eating, sleeping, she was forming His body from hers. His flesh and blood. From her humanity she gave Him His humanity.

Walking in the streets of Nazareth to do her shopping, to visit her friends, she set His feet on the path of Jerusalem.

Washing, weaving, kneading, sweeping, her hands prepared His hands for the nails.

Every beat of her heart gave Him His heart to love with, His heart to be broken by love.

All her experience of the world about her was gathered to Christ growing in her.   **Caryll Houselander**

Mary is the living mold of God.   **St. Augustine**

The child is like the parent. Mary was no mere instrument in God's dispensation; the Word of God did not merely come to her and go from her; He did not merely pass through her, as He may pass through us in Holy Communion; it was no heavenly body which the Eternal Son assumed, fashioned by the angels, and brought down to this lower world; no: He imbibed, He sucked up her blood and her substance into His Divine Person; He became man of her, and received her lineaments and her features, as the appearance and character under which He should manifest Himself to the world. He was known, doubtless, by His likeness to her, to be her Son.   **Cardinal John Henry Newman**

And Mary said,
"My soul magnifies the Lord,
    and my spirit rejoices in God my Savior,
        for he has regarded the low estate of his
            handmaiden.

For behold, henceforth all generations will call
   me blessed;
for he who is mighty has done great things for me,
   and holy is his name.
And his mercy is on those who fear him
   from generation to generation.
He has shown strength with his arm,
he has scattered the proud in the imagination of
      their hearts,
he has put down the mighty from their thrones,
   and exalted those of low degree;
he has filled the hungry with good things,
   and the rich he has sent empty away.
He has helped his servant Israel,
in remembrance of his mercy,
as he spoke to our fathers,
to Abraham and to his posterity for ever."

"The Magnificat" (Luke 1:46-55)

*For he who is mighty has done great things for me, and
holy is his name. The great things* are nothing less than
that she became the Mother of God, in which work
so many and such great good things are bestowed on
her as pass man's understanding. For on this there
follows all honor, all blessedness, and her unique
place in the whole of humankind, among which she
has no equal, namely, that she had a child by the
Father in heaven, and such a child.

   She herself is unable to find a name for this work,
it is too exceedingly great; all she can do is break out
in the fervent cry: "They are great things," impossi-

ble to describe or define. Hence men and women have crowned all her glory into a single word, calling her the Mother of God. No one can say anything greater of her or to her, though he had as many tongues as there are leaves on the trees, or grass in the fields, or stars in the sky, or sand by the sea. It needs to be pondered in the heart what it means to be the Mother of God.   **Martin Luther**

*Mary, help me to know more fully
the precious gift of a mother.
You always hear me when I call.
Embrace me with your loving care
and keep watch over my steps,
that Jesus may be born in me.
Through Christ our Lord. Amen.*

Mother and Child

She... wrapped him up in swaddling clothes, and laid him in a manger.

Only that. The brief sweet offices
Of motherhood: the gentleness that cared
Thus for a Child's small need: the simple, calm,
Unhastened task, that in the very words
The telling takes, is strong with humanness,
And sure with peace, and must forever keep
Him ours, and say forever she is ours.
Only that. No word of great travail,

No word of pain, or fright, or ecstasy,
No strangeness. Only that. The quiet hands
Wrapped him up in swaddling clothes, and laid
    him in a manger.

Her first gift then to Him, and His first witness
To the ways of earth, the first of tribute,
And the gesture that began the long
Fulfillment was a simple care she brought
To Him, not as a creature comes to stoop,
But as a mother bends to love.   John Lynch

Again, the scene is so very familiar: Mary and Joseph
forced to take shelter in a stable in Bethlehem, waiting for
the birth of their child. Great joy and wonder usually sur-
round the arrival of any new life. But what could have
been Mary's thoughts and feelings when she gave birth to
the very Son of the Most High God?

New responsibilities came with the birth of Jesus. Like
any young mother, Mary had to learn how to care for her
newborn baby. The months and years passed quickly as the
child grew in stature and wisdom. We can be sure that the
boy Jesus blessed his mother with countless joys, but each
step brought both him and Mary closer to the cross.

In those days a decree went out from Caesar
Augustus that all the world should be enrolled....
And Joseph also went up from Galilee, from the city
of Nazareth, to Judea, to the city of David, which is
called Bethlehem, because he was of the house and

lineage of David, to be enrolled with Mary, his be-trothed, who was with child. And while they were there, the time came for her to be delivered. And she gave birth to her first-born son and wrapped him in swaddling cloths, and laid him in a manger, because there was no place for them in the inn.   **Luke 2:1-7**

Mary, the Virgin Mother, brings forth today the Author of grace. She is the Mother and [Queen] of the universe; she remains a Virgin as she gives birth today to her Son. The sun begets the Sun; the crea-ture gives birth to the Creator. She is His child and she is His Mother. Mary was chosen as Mother, pre-destined before all creatures, filled with all grace, all virtue, all holiness, to the end that of a Mother most pure might be born the Son infinitely pure.

   And as in Heaven the Son has a Father immortal and eternal, so on earth the Son, according to the flesh, is like the Mother. In Heaven He is eternal and immense with the Father; on earth, like the Mother, He is in time and full of meekness. In Heaven He is the image of the Father; on earth He is the likeness of His Mother.   **St. Augustine**

A privilege of Mary is that she alone above all crea-tures was in the body most familiar with God. For, what was never granted to any other creature, nor will ever be granted again in eternity—she bore God for nine months in her womb, she nourished God from her breasts full of heaven, for many years she sweetly brought up Our Lord, she had God subject to her, she handled and embraced her God in pure embraces and kisses with tender familiarity.

St. Bonaventure

To feel God powerless in one's arms and to be able to minister to His wants would be, in itself, sufficient to bewilder any soul less strong and less simple than Mary's. She did not pass her time in motionless adoration. *Her maternal attentions to the needs of her Child were her worship. She never for an instant lost sight of the Babe in her adoration of her God, nor did her deep realization of the Godhead cause her to forget for a moment the necessities of the Child.*

The physical tie which bound her to Jesus, the natural maternal instincts which such a tie created, would make it impossible to lose sight of the fact that the Being that nestled in her arms and looked to her for help, protection and sustenance was her Child. The absolute independence of the God did not dim her perception and full realization of the complete dependence of the Babe.

But this profound sense of the reality of the Infancy of Jesus did not cloud her vision of the power and the glory and the divinity that lay hidden under the frail, fleshly envelope. Her mother's love became mingled and identified with the creature's most perfect love of its Creator. She had not two loves of Jesus in her heart, the love of a mother for her child and the love of a creature for its God. The latter simply passed into the former, undergoing, in the passage, a marked transformation. In the Mother's love for her Child, the creature's love of the Creator was touched with a marvelous devotedness, tenderness, and reverent familiarity.   **Edward Leen, C.S.Sp.**

To be the Mother of God is the greatest grace that can be conferred on a creature. It is such that God could make a greater world, a greater heaven, but that he cannot exalt a creature more than by making her his Mother.   **St. Bonaventure**

Whatever is wholesome and real and tender in a mother-child relationship existed between Mary and Jesus. She wrapped him in swaddling clothes and placed him in a manger. She counted his fingers and toes. She studied his eyes until the day she could tell he was able to see. She nursed him and held him and loved him.

Later she taught him to speak and delighted in his first words. He learned her accent, her intonation, her idiomatic expressions. She taught him the names of flowers and insects, the words of psalms. Through her, God the Father loved and comforted his Son when he was hurt by bruises or cut by rejection or loneliness. She looked down smiling with pleasure at this child she loved, until one day she found herself looking up into his face. He had grown up.

John Randall, S.T.D.

It is not fantastic to presume that since by his own will Christ as an infant received God's love through Mary, since it was she who clothed him, fed him, bathed him, taught him to walk and to speak, it was she too who first took him out into the fields to see the grass and the wild flowers and bade him keep as still as a mouse to watch the sparrows.

If we may guess that he was thinking of his mother when he began telling of his Father's love and how it is shown through flowers and birds, we may certainly be sure that he was thinking of her when he spoke of the mother hen gathering her chicks under her wings.

The images that he used evoke picture after picture of his home life. As you listen to him, you can almost see the grave little boy watching his mother with the absorbed interest that children always bring to skilled work beautifully done, watching her cook and sweep and bake, put the oil in the lamps, light the candles and bottle the wine.   **Caryll Houselander**

The real nature of a person is often most pronounced in childhood, and during Jesus' childhood Mary was privileged as no one else to observe something of His real self as the Son of God, for after all, He was her Child; He had been placed in her charge. She was closest to Him. More than anyone else she was permitted to gaze into His eyes. No doubt, He told her much of what was on His heart, and she was privileged to hear the most words from His lips.

Basilea Schlink

Mary's function in the Incarnation was not completed when Jesus was born. It was a continuous task, involving the human formation of the young man, as he grew up from infancy to childhood and from childhood to adulthood. How this was accomplished is hidden from us. Only Mary knew the secrets of Jesus' upbringing, and kept them in her heart. She, his mother, kept the secret of the first childish word her Child ever spoke to her and meditated [on] it in her heart. God, in his humanity, formed his first word, and there can be little doubt that it was "Mama."   **Edward Schillebeeckx, O.P.**

He was nursed and tended by her; he was suckled by her; he lay in her arms. As time went on, he ministered to her, and obeyed her. He lived with her for thirty years, in one house, with an uninterrupted intercourse, and with only the saintly Joseph to share it with him. She was the witness of his growth, of his joys, of his sorrows, of his prayers; she was blest with his smile, with the touch of his hand, with the whisper of his affection, with the expression of his thoughts and his feelings for that length of time. Now my brethren, what ought she to be, what is it *becoming* that she should be, who was so favored?

Cardinal John Henry Newman

Mary, help me to know more fully
the precious gift of a mother.
You always hear me when I call.
Embrace me with your loving care
and keep watch over my steps,

that Jesus may be born in me.
Through Christ our Lord. Amen.

Jesus Gives Us a Mother

When John this tale began to tell
Mary would not longer dwell
Till she came unto that hill
 There she might her own Son see.
  Mary Mother, come and see:
  Thy Son is nailed upon a tree.
O my sweet Son, thou art me dear.
Why have men hangyd Thee here?
Thy head is closyd with a briar.
 Why have men done so to Thee.
  Mary Mother, come and see:
  Thy Son is nailed upon a tree.
John, this woman thee betake.
Keep this woman for My sake.
On rood I hang for mannys sake,
 For sinful man, as thou may see.
  Mary Mother, come and see:
  Thy Son is nailed upon a tree.
                    Anonymous English Carol

Jesus loved us to the end. His last earthly deed was to give his mother to John, his beloved disciple, and thus to each of us. This gift is a signal expression of God's love for us all. Do we realize how precious is this gift of a mother?

But standing by the cross of Jesus were his mother, and his mother's sister, Mary the wife of Clopas, and Mary Magdalene. When Jesus saw his mother, and the disciple whom he loved standing near, he said to his mother, "Woman, behold, your son!" Then he said to the disciple, "Behold, your mother!" And from that hour the disciple took her to his own home. After this Jesus, knowing that all was now finished, said (to fulfill the scripture), "I thirst." **John 19:25-28**

The principal actor in this scene is Jesus himself. The central action is Jesus' transfer of gifts—Mary to the disciple, the disciple to Mary. During his ministry Jesus bestowed many gifts: his word, his signs, the Eucharist, the revelation of the Father. As a person in the shadow of impending death gives away, one by one, his personal treasures to the survivors whom he loves most dearly, so does Jesus at his "hour." It is his final gift before he dies, given with utter freedom. The soldiers take his clothes and divide them; it was not his choice who would receive them. Not so with the gift of his mother, Jesus' last initiative before he breathes his last. His mother is not taken from him; he gives her away. **George Montague, S.M.**

Standing at the foot of the cross, utterly spent, in agony, Mary is an empty vessel and the Spirit is praying in her. Then Jesus speaks giving her a new command, a new call, "Woman, this is your son," and down through the years Mary's heart echoes, "I am the handmaid of the Lord. Let what you say be done." She agrees to go on living. She will not die no matter how much she craves to go home to her Father, to her husband, Joseph, and to be reunited with her dying son. She will live, because that is the will of her Father.

The infant Church needed her. We are told she lived about twenty-five years after Jesus died and rose. The Church was a quarter of a century old before the mother of the Church was called to go home to her Father's house. **John Randall, S.T.D.**

The Redeemer entrusts his mother to the disciple, and at the same time he gives her to him as his mother. Mary's motherhood, which becomes man's inheritance, is a gift: *a gift which Christ himself makes* personally to every individual. The Redeemer entrusts Mary to John because he entrusts John to Mary. At the foot of the Cross there begins that special *entrusting of humanity to the Mother of Christ....*

Pope John Paul II, *Redemptoris Mater*

It is clear that Jesus' confiding of Mary to the beloved disciple is not merely a son's provision for his mother's care after his death. What Jesus does here is the fulfillment of prophecy, for the very next verse states that Jesus "seeing now that all things had been accomplished..." (John 19:28). The unusual title "Woman" by which Jesus addresses his mother leads us to the woman of Genesis 3:15, which spoke of the "seed" of the woman who would engage Satan.

But the prophecies which the announcement of Jesus most clearly fulfill are those foretelling the generation of the new people of God by mother Jerusalem. The surprise is that the fulfillment goes beyond expectations, for there is a real human mother who fulfills the promises, who is Jerusalem in person.

George Montague, S.M.

Together with Mary, and under her influence, we encounter Christ the man directly. He in turn leads us to the Father. In this sense it is better to think of Christ as giving Mary to us as our Mother, rather than of Mary as giving us Christ—"Behold thy mother." He freely chose his mother and ours for himself and for all of us.... **Edward Schillebeeckx, O.P.**

If only you recognized God's gift, said Jesus to the Samaritan woman. In this gift is enclosed the gift of Mary, for the mystery of the Son encompasses that of his Mother. One must not hesitate to accept from the hands of God what we are thus offered. To each one of us God repeats in some way the angel's words to Joseph: *Have no fear about taking Mary as your wife. It is by the Holy Spirit that she has conceived this child.* It is necessary to receive this gift from above with humility: to welcome, with open heart, all the love of God invested in Mary, for her joy and ours.

Cardinal Léon Joseph Suenens

Mary, help me to know more fully
the precious gift of a mother.
You always hear me when I call.
Embrace me with your loving care
and keep watch over my steps,
that Jesus may be born in me.
Through Christ our Lord. Amen.

Mother by Grace

O Mother of fair love, it was not alone
Christ whom you mothered on the first Christmas
    night,
not alone the Orient, the Splendor that outshone
daylight and suns and all created light.
It was not only this new dearness, kissed and held
in love and lullabies among the straw,
warmed by the breath of oxen that still smelled
of clover and sweet fields. But in deep awe
there crept in with the shepherd and his sheep
and bowed down with the Oriental king
your other children who will always keep
the joy of your mysterious mothering,
cause of our joy, heaven's gate, at once our mother,
on that first Christmas night, through Christ, our
    Brother.   **"Cause of Our Joy" by Sister Maris Stella**

From the moment Christ told Mary to take John as her
Son, she opened her heart to all the world and became our

spiritual mother. Through her mother's eyes she sees each one of us the way she sees Jesus, her only Son. She has adopted us as brothers and sisters of Christ, and loves each of us as her very own children, begotten by grace.

"I will not leave you orphans," Jesus said (John 14:18). An orphan has neither father nor mother. Jesus gave us both: "No one has ever seen God. The only Son, who is at the Father's side, has revealed him" (John 1:18). And: "Behold your mother" (John 19:27). We can live as orphans if we choose. But we can also claim our birthright and live as children nurtured to fullness by a father's and a mother's love.

George Montague, S.M.

The gentleness that floods our heart when we see a woman with child floods Our Lady's heart when she looks down upon the world, for through her the Holy Spirit has made humanity large with the Christ-child, and she, who is so essentially ours, who is one of the human race, is compelled with us in the mutual tenderness which can have but one answer: "Little children, love one another."

The Christhood that she recognizes in us is that we are her children: "Mother, behold your child."

This is the most wonderful trust of all, which Christ has given to us, to be Himself to Our Lady. He has actually given *His* love for her into our keeping. We are trustees of His love in our love for one another; He has given us His heart to give to the Bride of Life. **Caryll Houselander**

Mary is our mother in the supernatural order. She is really and truly our mother, just as much so as is our mother in the natural order.

A mother is one who gives life. Our earthly mother gave us our life in this world, our natural life. Mary has given us the life that elevates our life in this world and flowers in the next, our supernatural life.

Don Sharkey

The divine motherhood of the blessed Virgin is therefore God's grace alone, and her own act, inseparably. It is not simply a physical motherhood, it is her grace and her deed, placing her whole self, body and soul, at the service of God and his redemptive mercy to mankind. **Karl Rahner**

It is very, very important for us to have a deep love for our Lady. For she was the one who taught Jesus how to walk, how to pray, how to wash, how to do all the little things that make our human life so beautiful. She had to do them. And the same thing now— she will always be willing to help us and teach us how to be all for Jesus alone, how to love only Jesus, how to touch him and see him, to serve him in the distressing disguise. **Mother Teresa of Calcutta**

Now from the Calvary scene it is clear that Mary, the Mother of Jesus, is part of those treasures of Jesus that the Holy Spirit unwraps. One must, of course, be open to the gift and prayer is the way to that openness. Have you ever consciously received Mary as your mother? Have you ever consciously said "Yes" to this gift? Far from being a threat to Jesus, when you receive his gifts, you receive him in a deeper way....

Mary is clearly one of the gifts of Jesus. To welcome her as our mother is to receive the consecrating action of God. We enter more deeply into the holiness of God by accepting this gift. The bond which God establishes between Mary and us, a bond of mother and child, when affirmed and accepted by us, is a new and deeper consecration of ourselves to God. **George Montague, S.M.**

Realize that none of us stands before the cross alone. Mary is always there, ever faithful, ever mindful of our need to accept whatever form the cross takes in our own lives. She is our Mother of Sorrows, her face a magnificent portrait of compassion. Dwell on her face. Absorb her expression. She does not clutch sorrow like some dark possession brewing hatred, depression or revenge. Her sorrow is a selfless thing, a pure reflection of her Son's forgiving love.

Hear the voice of Jesus speaking to you: "Behold your Mother."

Let the healing power of his words penetrate you.

Accept his gift, accept its consoling reality. Mary is not some heavenly being appointed to act as a mother toward you. She is wholly human and wholly your Mother. Through her, Jesus realizes the joy of mothering you, bringing you gradually and surely into the fullness of faith.

Be silent before Mary and hear her. **Gloria Hutchinson**

Catherine Labouré never forgot a certain sensation that occurred when Our Lady appeared to her in 1830 in Paris. Catherine had lost her own mother at the age of nine. When the radiant and exquisite Virgin sat down in a chair in the sanctuary of the convent chapel, the young nun dropped to her knees in front of her. But then the needs of a daughter's heart took over. She placed her hands on the silk-robed knees. It was the understandable response of a devoted daughter. "I am sure that this was the happiest moment of my life," she wrote twenty-six years later. **Catherine Odell**

How happy my soul was, good Mother, when I had the good fortune to gaze upon you! How I love to recall the pleasant moments spent under your gaze, so full of kindness and mercy for us. Yes, tender Mother, you stooped down to earth to appear to a mere child.... You, the Queen of heaven and earth, deigned to make use of the most fragile thing in the world's eyes. **St. Bernadette**

I remember that when my mother died I was twelve years old or a little less. When I began to understand what I had lost, I went afflicted before an image of Our Lady and besought her with many tears to be my mother. It seems to me that although I did this in simplicity it helped me. For I have found favor with this sovereign Virgin in everything I have asked of her and in the end she has drawn me to herself.

St. Teresa of Avila

Oh, how delightful and profitable it is to be visited by this holy Lady, for her visit always brings us many blessings. "O God," you will say, "I do wish the Virgin would visit me!" And why? "To be consoled, for it is so pleasant to have consolations! I would so love to have an ecstasy, a ravishment; indeed, I would very much like this sacred Virgin to show herself to me." Yes, and would you receive her as St. Elizabeth received her? Our Lady comes to visit us very often but we do not really want to receive her.

St. Francis de Sales

Mary, help me to know more fully
the precious gift of a mother.
You always hear me when I call.
Embrace me with your loving care
and keep watch over my steps,
that Jesus may be born in me.
Through Christ our Lord. Amen.

A Mother's Personal Love and Care

The gentle hands of Mary, God's mother,
Pick up each mutilated little corpse
Abortion brought.
She unbuttons the red cloak.
Its lining is white like Her virginal soul.
She takes the little bodies
And gently buries them in a nice field;
And as She does,
The daisies and other field flowers
Decorate and cover the endless little graves.
But oh! the souls of the little corpses
She takes into Her mantle lined with white,
And, like a Mother, holds them tight.

Catherine de Hueck Doherty

*How does Mary express a mother's tender love and care
toward us? Indeed, how can she love us at all, seeing so
clearly our wretched sinfulness? We shall see in these
meditations that Mary bends over us, follows us step by
step, and knows our smallest needs before we even think to
bring them to our mother.*

Mary receives power to look upon us, each and all,
with a mother's watchfulness. Lost in God by means
of the beatific vision, she yet knows us, one by one,
by name, and knows the whole story of each one's
life…. She sees us with all our miseries and loves us,

with a love which she receives from Him, at the very root of our being and the source whence we were born. It is a knowledge incomparably more penetrating than any other, a love which reaches to the deepest intimacy, a motherhood which nourishes us drop by drop to maturity.   **Cardinal Léon Joseph Suenens**

The Blessed Virgin continues to be the loving consoler of humanity in the many physical and moral sufferings that afflict and torment it. She knows our sorrows and our griefs, because she, too, suffered from Bethlehem to Calvary: "And a sword will pierce through your own soul too" (Luke 2:35). Mary is our spiritual Mother, and a mother who always understands her own children and consoles them in their troubles.   **Pope John Paul II**

The Blessed Virgin Mary offers a calm vision and a reassuring word to modern man, torn as he often is between anguish and hope, defeated by the sense of his own limitations, troubled in his mind and divided in his heart, uncertain before the riddle of death, oppressed by loneliness while yearning for fellowship.

Mary shows forth the victory of hope over anguish, of fellowship over solitude, of eternal visions over earthly ones, of life over death.   **Pope Paul VI**

Like the Church of which she is a model, Mary is the mother of all who are born again to a new life. She is the mother of him who is the Life by which all things live; when she bore him, she gave new birth in a sense to all who were to live by his life.

Recognizing that by virtue of this mystery she is the mother of all Christians, Christ's blessed mother also shows herself a mother to them by her care and loving kindness. She never grows hard toward her children, as though they were not her own. The womb that once gave birth is not dried up; it continues to bring forth the fruit of her tender compassion.

Blessed Guerric of Igny

We need only show Mary the wounds of our souls, and she immediately helps us by her prayers, and consoles us.   **St. Alphonsus**

The love that this good mother bears us is so great that as soon as she perceives our want, she comes to our assistance. She comes before she is called.

Richard of St. Laurence

Let Christians run to Mary with confidence in all their temptations and in all their needs: for no one has anything to fear, no one can despair of the success of any enterprise with her for guide, for patron, for shield, for protectress. She loves us with a mother's love. She takes upon herself the burden of our salvation.   **Pope Pius IX**

The love of our mother will be the breath that kindles into a living flame the embers of virtue that are hidden under the ashes of your indifference.

Josemaria Escriva de Balaguer

It is a great comfort on our spiritual way, which is often fatiguing and bristling with difficulties, to meet the gentle presence of a mother. One is so at ease near one's mother. With her, everything becomes easier; the weary, discouraged heart, disturbed by storms, finds new hope and strength, and continues the journey with fresh courage.

Gabriel of St. Mary Magdalen, O.C.D.

Every trifling thing is told to her and every great sorrow; she is the sharer of all earth's joys and griefs.

She is not wearied with our littleness; her smile comes down to us like a benediction through the sea of flickering candles, and she blesses our wild flowers withering at her feet. For each one of us is "another Christ"; each one, to Mary, is her only child. It is therefore not tedious to her to hear the trifles that we tell her, to look at the bruises that we bring to her, and seeing our wound of sin, to [bring it to her Son for healing]. **Caryll Houselander**

The Heart of Mary is so tender towards us, that the hearts of all mothers in the world put together cannot be compared to hers. All that the Son asks the Father is granted Him. All that the Mother asks of the Son is in like manner granted to her. **St. John Vianney**

Mary is so kind and courteous that she is ever with us; keeps us company in solitude; accompanies us on our journeys; counsels us in doubt; consoles us in affliction; assists us in sickness; defends us from our enemies, visible and invisible; encourages us in fear; and protects us from the anger and vengeance of God.

If we call her, she answers promptly; if we salute her, she courteously returns the salutation; if we praise her, she kindly thanks us; if we do her any service, she abundantly reimburses us; if we show her faith and love, she gives us the most tender proofs of her affection.   ***Day by Day With My Daily Visitor***

And so we will have recourse to this exalted Mother with all the enthusiasm and filial love of which we are capable, and we will show her our trust in particular. Do you have trust in Mary? Do you confide in her? Do you tell her your troubles? Do you present your expectations and your hopes to her? Do you really look to her as the dispenser of goodness, of help, of kindness, of Christian fellowship?

Let us think about the indescribable good fortune of being able to call her Mother, of being related to her. There is no distance between Mary and us. Instead we share the child's habit of turning to his mother at every moment and telling her everything.

Pope Paul VI

Mary, help me to know more fully
the precious gift of a mother.
You always hear me when I call.
Embrace me with your loving care
and keep watch over my steps,

that Jesus may be born in me.
Through Christ our Lord. Amen.

A Mother's Watchful Eye

She always leaned to watch for us,
    Anxious if we were late,
In winter by the window,
    In summer by the gate.

And though we mocked her tenderly,
    Who had such foolish care,
The long way home would seem more safe
    Because she waited there.

Her thoughts were all so full of us—
    She never could forget!
And so I think that where she is
    She must be watching yet,

Waiting till we come home to her,
    Anxious if we are late—
Watching from heaven's window,
    Leaning from heaven's gate.   **"The Watcher"**
                                    by Margaret Widdemer

An important element of Mary's tender, loving care is expressed in the many ways she guards us from dangers of every sort on our journey toward full union with her Son. How does Mary personally protect and guide each of us as we struggle to reach the safe harbor of eternity?

We find ourselves in this earth as in a tempestuous sea, in a desert, in a vale of tears. Now then, Mary is the Star of the Sea, the solace of our desert, the light that guides us towards Heaven. **St. John Bosco**

Mary is called the Star of the Sea because, as St. Thomas says, *even as sailors are guided into port by means of a star, so Christians are guided towards Heaven by means of Mary.* This absolute guarantee of the protection of our heavenly Mother should increase our trust in her and lead us to turn towards her in every difficulty and temptation. **Cardinal Antonio Bacci**

Turn not away your eyes from the splendor of this star, if you will not be overwhelmed by storms. If the winds of temptation arise, if you strike on the rocks of temptation, or tribulation, look upon the star, call on Mary.... If you follow her guidance, you will not go astray. If you pray to her, you will not give up hope. If you think of her, you will not go wrong. If she upholds you, you will not stumble. If she protects you, you will not be afraid. If she leads you, you will reach the goal. **St. Bernard**

The Virgin always protects us. She is the cause of our joy, and we try to be a cause for her joy. Thus gathered, following her example, invoking her protection, staying united with her, we can move through the most difficult places with no fear at all because

Jesus is with us and he will never abandon us: Jesus is our love, our strength, our source of kindness.

Mother Teresa of Calcutta

What shall bring me forward in the narrow way, as I live in the world, but the thought and patronage of Mary? What shall seal my senses, shall tranquilize my heart, when sights and sounds of danger are around me but Mary? What shall give me patience and endurance, when I am wearied out with the length of the conflict with evil, with the unceasing necessity of precautions, with the irksomeness of observing them, with the tediousness of their reception, with the strain upon my mind, with my forlorn and cheerless condition, but a loving communion with you!

You will comfort me in my discouragements, solace me in my fatigues, raise me after my falls, reward me for my successes. You will show me your Son, my God and my all. When my spirit within me is excited, or relaxed, or depressed, when it loses its balance, when it is restless and wayward, when it is sick of what it has, and hankers after what it has not, when my eye is solicited with evil and my mortal frame trembles under the shadow of the tempter, what will bring me to myself, to peace and health, but the cool breath of the Immaculate and the fragrance of the Rose of Sharon?

Cardinal John Henry Newman

Mother! Call her with a loud voice. She is listening to you; she sees you in danger, perhaps, and she—your holy mother Mary—offers you, along with the grace of her son, the refuge of her arms, the tenderness of her embrace... and you will find yourself with added strength for the new battle.

Josemaria Escriva de Balaguer

It can be seen that the children themselves recognize her as their mother. A natural instinct, inspired by faith, prompts them to have recourse to her in all dangers and difficulties, invoking her and taking refuge in her arms like little ones running to their mother. To this day we dwell in the shelter of the mother of the Most High, remaining under her protection as it were beneath the shadow of her wings. And in the days to come we shall share in her glory; we shall know the warmth of her loving embrace. Then there will be one joyful voice proclaiming the praise of our mother: Holy Mother of God, *in you we all find our home!*   **Blessed Guerric of Igny**

Pope John Paul II was shot three times at close range by a trained assassin at St. Peter's Square in Rome on May 13, 1981—the anniversary of the apparition of the Virgin Mary at Fatima. The fact that he was only wounded and not killed, the Pope attributes to the special protection of Our Lady of Fatima. It was later reported that had the twenty-five minute ride to the hospital taken five minutes longer, the Pope would have bled to death. Or if one of the bullets had come only a fraction of an inch closer to some vital organ, he would have died. The Pope himself expressed his appreciation during an audience nearly five months after the shooting:

And again I have become indebted to the Blessed Virgin and to all the Patron Saints. Could I forget that the event in Saint Peter's Square took place on the day and at the hour when the first appearance of the Mother of Christ to the poor little peasants has been remembered for over sixty years at Fatima in Portugal? For in everything that happened to me on that very day, I felt that extraordinary protection and care, which turned out to be stronger than the deadly bullet. **Pope John Paul II**

*Mary, help me to know more fully
the precious gift of a mother.
You always hear me when I call.
Embrace me with your loving care
and keep watch over my steps,
that Jesus may be born in me.
Through Christ our Lord. Amen.*

TWO

The Model Disciple

Mary is the model disciple, the one human being—next to the Lord Jesus Christ himself, who is both human and divine—who most perfectly loved and served God and her neighbors with her whole heart, her whole mind, and her whole soul. Her purity of heart shines as an example for every follower of Christ.

Pure of Heart

This, could I paint my inward sight,
This were Our Lady of the Night:
She bears on her front's lucency
The starlight of her purity:
For as the white rays of that star
The union of all colors are,
She sums all virtues that may be

In her sweet light of purity.
The mantle which she holds on high
Is the great mantle of the sky.
Think, o sick toiler, when the night
Comes on thee, sad and infinite.

Think, sometimes, 'tis our own Lady
Spreads her own mantle over thee,
And folds the earth, a wearied thing,
Beneath its gentle shadowing.
Then rest a little; and in sleep
Forget to weep, forget to weep!

**"Lines for a Drawing of Our Lady of the Night"
by Francis Thompson**

It was only fitting that the Virgin to whose care God the Father was pleased to confide His only Son, should shine with a dazzling purity, surpassing all but that of God Himself.   **St. Anselm**

Mary was such, that her life alone was a model for all. Let the virginity and life of Mary be to you as a faithful image, in which the form of virtue is resplendent.

St. Ambrose

If you look diligently at Mary, there is nothing of virtue, nothing of beauty, nothing of splendor or glory which does not shine in her.   **St. Jerome**

Mary was more blessed because God was born spiritually in her soul than because he was born from her in the flesh.   **St. Augustine**

Of herself, Mary is nothing, even as all other creatures are; but by God's gift she is the most perfect of creatures, the most perfect image of God's divine being in a purely human creature. **St. Maximilian Kolbe**

No one has ever more perfectly contained the light of God than Mary who by the perfection of her purity and humility is, as it were, completely identified with truth like the clean window pane which vanishes entirely into the light which it transmits. The Church celebrates, in Mary, the perfect rekindling of the pure light which had been extinguished by the sin of Adam. In Mary, the lamp was once more perfectly clean, burning with pure light, standing on the lampstand, illuminating the whole house of God, restoring meaning to all God's creatures, and showing the rest of men the way to return to the light.

Thomas Merton

As a diamond reflects all light, Mary who, according to God's plan, had been chosen to be the "Dawn of Salvation," faithfully reflected all the graces received from the Holy Spirit, without keeping anything for herself. **Cardinal Léon Joseph Suenens**

For as the dawn is the end of night, and the beginning of day, well may the Blessed Virgin Mary, who was the end of vices, be called the dawn of day.

Pope Innocent III

What are all the maidservants, manservants, gentle-men, ladies, princes, kings, monarchs on earth compared with the Virgin Mary, who is of royal lineage and, moreover, the Mother of God, the noblest lady on earth? After Christ she is the fairest gem in all of Christendom. Never can she be praised enough: the supreme empress and queen, far exalted above all nobility, wisdom, and holiness.   **Martin Luther**

She was a virgin not only in body but also in mind, who stained the sincerity of its disposition by no guile, who was humble in heart, grave in speech, prudent in mind, sparing of words, studious in reading, resting her hope not on uncertain riches, but on the prayer of the poor, intent on work, modest in discourse; wont to seek not man but God as the judge of her thoughts, to injure no one, to have good-will towards all, to rise up before her elders, not to envy her equals, to avoid boastfulness, to follow reason, to love virtue.   **St. Ambrose**

In Mary we see that in His wisdom and goodness God has given us the model of all the virtues which we can imitate. As we look upon her and think about her we do not feel as it were dazzled by the brilliance of God but, on the contrary, drawn by the kinship of a nature we share in common with her, we strive with greater confidence to imitate her.   **Pope Leo XIII**

What confers upon Mary her peerless rank is her capacity for corresponding to the divine love; the abyss she offers to that divine outpouring. No creature, angelic or human, can receive that love as she can; not one has corresponded as she has to the divine advances. She is wholly surrendered to God's good pleasure, and in her he has been able to realize the perfect work of his creation.

Cardinal Léon Joseph Suenens

The Church knows that in this praise of Mary's singleness, she is not ascribing to Mary an excellence which she acquired by her own power, and which would give her rights in relation to God. The Church is only praising in this way the pure and dazzling mercy of God.   **Karl Rahner**

Holiness was required in dealing with the holy things of God. But with the mother Mary far more was involved than rites and offerings prefiguring what was to come. She was privileged to bear Jesus Himself within her. After being touched by the Holiest of all, Mary would have kept herself pure in the spiritual sense, with her innermost self immersed in the stillness of God's holy presence.

But even beforehand she must have lived in this state, for God usually prepares and trains His instruments long in advance, as He did with a man like Moses. How else could such chosen instruments of the Lord come into close contact with the divine and God Himself. He is a consuming fire and never draws near to us unless He has first cleansed us and purged us of our sins (Isaiah 6).   **Basilea Schlink**

In Mary's Immaculate Conception the realities that bind men to God—creation, elevation, grace, redemption—attain their greatest realization in a pure creature. In the light of Mary's sanctity can the devastation caused by sin most accurately be gauged.

Ferrer Smith, O.P.

In Mary, the Immaculate Mother of God, we learn that a saint's mission in the world is often not revealed to the world till after death. The starry firmament took time to lay bare all its secrets, and as the centuries went by, star by star the gems were set in the royal crown of God's Mother, and more and more brightly her figure shone down upon Christ's Body, drawing to it all who sought purity and holiness, sighing to be saved from the threadbare illusions of an unstable world; all who with their last gasp sought to disentangle themselves, escape at the last minute from the equivocal spirit of the world.

Josef Weiger

Mary was the first personal realization of what awaits the redeemed. She is that still, but the distances have been done away with. The Church continues to look at Mary in Christ, but in a different way: no longer as its future and as a token of its hope, but only as the summit of its communion in Christ. The Church used to look at Mary as a fleet in the storm looks at the first ship which has crossed the bar and reached port. Now, the Church has rejoined her at the end of the voyage. There is no longer either separation or distance, but common joy in reunion in Christ. **René Laurentin**

> *Mary, your example of purity,*
> *faith, and humble obedience*
> *inspires me to be a better disciple.*
> *Pray for me in the midst of difficulties,*
> *that I may always follow your Son, Jesus,*
> *and love God with all my heart.*
> *Through Christ our Lord. Amen.*

Meek and Lowly

I am not proud—meek angels ye invest
New meeknesses to hear such utterance rest
On mortal lips—'I am not proud'—not proud!
Albeit in my flesh God sent His Son.
Albeit over Him my head is bowed
As others bow before Him, still mine heart
Bends lower than their knees. O centuries
That roll, in vision, your futurities
   My future grace athwart—
Whose murmurs seem to reach me while I keep
   Watch o'er this sleep—
Say of me as the Heavenly said—'Thou art
The blessedest of women!'—blessedest,
Not holiest, not noblest—no high name,
Whose height misplaced may pierce me
   like a shame,
When I sit meek in heaven!

For me—for me—
God knows that I am feeble like the rest!
I often wandered forth, more child than maiden,
Among the midnight hills of Galilee,
　Whose summits looked heaven-laden;
Listening to silence as it seemed to be
God's voice, so soft yet strong—so fain to press
Upon my heart as heaven did on the height,
And waken up its shadows by a light,
And show its vileness by a holiness.
Then I knelt down most silent like the night,
　Too self-renounced for fears,
Raising my small face to the boundless blue
Whose stars did mix and tremble in my tears.
God heard them falling after—with his dew.

"The Virgin Mary to the Child Jesus"
by Elizabeth Barrett Browning

Even though gifted with unparalleled purity in body, mind, and spirit, Mary did not grow prideful. She humbly continued her simple tasks as wife and mother even in the midst of blessings too wonderful to describe. Yet, how quickly do we take on airs of superiority whenever we receive any special recognition? What can we learn about humility from this most humble of disciples?

Mary's Canticle is a song of affirmation. Mary wholly accepts herself for who and what she is. Honestly and happily she admits to being humble. Boldly but truthfully she announces an "unthinkable" prophecy: "All ages shall call me blessed!"... Being humble, Mary acknowledges, in the same breath, the source of her uniqueness and holiness: "God has done great things for me." She realizes God "raises the lowly to high places." Her lowliness has won her God's favor. *Day by Day With My Daily Visitor*

Though she pleased by her virginity, she conceived by her humility. **St. Bernard**

Mary's humility became a heavenly ladder, by which God came into the world. **St. Augustine**

St. Bernard says: "It is not hard to be humble in a hidden life, but to remain so in the midst of honors is a truly rare and beautiful virtue." The Blessed Virgin was certainly the woman whom God honored most highly, whom He raised above all other creatures; yet no creature was so humble and lowly as she. A holy rivalry seemed to exist between Mary and God; the higher God elevated her, the lowlier she became in her humility. **Gabriel of St. Mary Magdalen, O.C.D.**

Mary could not have humbled herself more than she did humble herself in the Incarnation of the Word; God could not have exalted Mary more than he did exalt her. **St. Alphonsus**

It was fitting that Christ should choose a little and humble woman, hardly more than a child, to be his mother, to give him to us; to reveal his way with us.

Mary knew that, knew so well that her humility revealed his glory and the immensity of his love more truly than any greatness could do. She exalted in her littleness and then forgot it, because it led her to the thought of him and that possessed her entirely.   **Caryll Houselander**

Unlike Eve, whose pride forced Adam to wield the hand of authority, the Woman breaks through the clouds of sin like the soft rays of the sun—penetrating and coloring everything they touch, but never casting a shadow over the sun.   **Mother Angelica**

Humility has a bad name. Many dismiss it as a perpetual hanging of the head, the coward's one claim to virtue. But humility is not that. The materialist who confesses he is only a soulless animal is not humbler than Mary of Nazareth, who knew she was a child of God. His thoughts are lofty, and she is humble. That is because her thoughts are true. She knew that her goodness, her greatness, came altogether from the great God, and she acted accordingly. Humility means acting upon the truth about God and ourselves. It is the proud man who hangs his head; otherwise, he would see God above him.

Fr. Payton's Rosary Prayer Book

No one has learned so well the lesson of humility as Mary did. She, being the handmaid of the Lord, was completely empty of self, and God filled her with grace. "Full of grace" means full of God. A handmaid is at someone's disposal, to be used according to someone's wish with full trust and joy, to belong to someone without reserve.   **Mother Teresa of Calcutta**

Because Mary did not mistrust the love of God, she could reply in the affirmative. From the depths of her being she could sense who God is and what He is like, so well, in fact, that she had not the slightest doubt that what He said to her through the angel was good and right. As a humble handmaiden she followed this unique leading of His in obedience. A humble person can believe. Because he does not trust in himself or have a high opinion of himself, he has to look to God for everything. He who is conscious of his weakness will find that his eyes are opened to God in His omnipotence.   **Basilea Schlink**

She did not even reveal her great secret to St. Joseph; she did not even speak to defend herself against the otherwise very plausible charge of adultery.

The later events of her life are of the same tone. She never sought for, never gained recognition for herself. When her Son was triumphantly offered Kingship by the crowds, there is no mention of her. But she did step forth from the shadows of modest retirement into the deep blackness of Calvary, after the Apostles, the sharers in His acclaim, had fled. She willingly took part in His disgrace, His shame, His rejection.

She not only did not seek recognition: she gladly accepted non-recognition, even disgrace.

William G. Most

In her own life, Mary appeared as the humble servant exalted in her humility by God. She exemplifies the paradox of grace that touches those who cannot accomplish anything by themselves. She personifies the Church of the poor, the Church that moves through history as a humble servant, and by that very fact is in a position to express the mystery of God's promise and proximity. **Cardinal Joseph Ratzinger**

Mary's life is always the same, simple and hidden, profoundly humble and modest. Modesty was a characteristic of her piety, of her virtues, and of all her actions.... Mary was the most humble of all creatures; consequently in heaven she is now the most glorious. If she is seated on the throne nearest to that of her Divine Son, it is because she approached nearer than any other to the perfection of His humility.

St. Peter Julian Eymard

But isn't it paradoxical that in her own lifetime, she who was part of the Promise, she whose heel would crush the tempter's head, she who was foreshadowed by Sarah, Judith, Esther, women who were the bright glory of Israel, she who was indeed the second

Eve, Mother of all the living, was to be unknown, the silent Virgin, the Mother of Sorrows? She made no figure in this world at all; she was almost anonymous; just "the child and his mother" (Matthew 2:14). And then, through the centuries, she was destined by God to grow in the mind and heart of the Church; to become closer and more real to mankind; to grow to be a living personal Queen and Mother to each one of us.   **Alban Boultwood**

> *Mary, your example of purity,*
> *faith, and humble obedience*
> *inspires me to be a better disciple.*
> *Pray for me in the midst of difficulties,*
> *that I may always follow your Son, Jesus,*
> *and love God with all my heart.*
> *Through Christ our Lord. Amen.*

Full of Faith

Mary's faith surpassed that of all men and all angels.
She saw her Son in the stable at Bethlehem and yet
  believed that He was the creator of the world.
She saw Him fleeing before Herod, and she never
  wavered in her faith that He was the King of
    Kings.
She saw Him being born, and she believed that
  He was from everlasting.

She saw Him poor, without even elemental
    necessities, and nevertheless believed Him to be
       the Master of the universe.
She saw Him lying on straw in the crib and there
    adored Him as the all-powerful One.
She saw that He spoke not a word, yet she believed
    that He was the eternal Wisdom itself.
She heard Him cry, and she believed that He was
    the joy of Paradise.
And in the end she saw Him die, exposed to all
    manner of insult, affixed to a cross, and though
       the faith of others was shaken,
Yet Mary persevered in her unhesitating belief that
    He was God.   **St. Alphonsus**

*What faith Mary must have had! To believe that she
would bear the Son of God? To believe that this helpless
infant was her creator? To believe that Jesus crucified was
the all-powerful God? Have you ever tried putting yourself into Mary's shoes, imagining how you might have
replied to the awesome message of the Archangel Gabriel?
Even when Mary did not understand God's word, she did
not let go of it but pondered that word until the intended
fruit was brought forth.*

As the Annunciation scene opens we find a startled
young virgin: startled to hear of her dignity, startled
to hear of her call. In the wonderful moment of faith
awakening who is not startled? When it first comes

upon us, whether in a sudden crash, a bolt of lightning, a mighty wind or the murmur of a gentle breeze, this new realization cuts right through all the previous constructs of our self-identity. "Me—the well-beloved of God? Me—a partaker of divinity, truly one with Christ, the Son? Me—called to be perfect, even as the heavenly Father is perfect?"

The only response we can make is that modeled for us by Mary: "But how can this be? How are you going to bring it about?" There are problems, there are difficulties; humanly speaking, there are even impossibilities. Of myself I can only be a sterile field. How can I become pregnant with divine life? From whence will come the life-giving seed so that Christ will be formed in me, so that I will truly be another Christ, a perfectly responsive son of God?

M. Basil Pennington, O.C.S.O.

Our faith in the Incarnation has, alas, a kind of remote, impersonal quality, whereas to Mary's faith that God would become man, there was added the piercing personal precision that this Incarnation was to take place in the child of her own body. We imagine, perhaps, the joy of her motherhood; and this joy was indeed to come, and to grow daily in her with her child, to be experienced most sweetly in his birth; but that first moment, as the angel offered the divine proposal, was surely one of supreme and heroic faith. We wrong Our Lady if we do not recognize her act of that strong, austere virtue; for surely hers was the greatest act of faith ever given God by human kind. **Alban Boultwood**

When Mary consented to the Incarnation of the Eternal Word, by means of her faith she opened heaven to men. **St. Augustine**

By believing and obeying, she begot the very Son of the Father on earth. She did not know man, but was overshadowed by the Holy Spirit, and, as the New Eve, she put her doubt-free faith in the messenger of God, not in the ancient serpent. She brought forth a Son whom God made the first-born among many brothers, that is, the faithful, in whose birth and development she cooperates with a motherly love.

Vatican II, "Dogmatic Constitution on the Church," no. 61

Never before had a person been required to believe what Mary was supposed to believe: that God would overrule His laws of nature concerning conception and birth, and in the manner foretold by the angel, assume human flesh in her. What an impossibility!

Mary, more than anyone else, was required to believe in a promise of God in defiance of all human reason.

This path of faith demanded exceptional courage and determination on Mary's part. And there was no one with whom she could talk, no one who could give her advice. She found herself far removed from every sphere of human experience. All she could do was cleave to God, to whom she was bound by the promise.   **Basilea Schlink**

Mary had to live by faith as we do. Reflect for a moment on the gigantic leap in faith that was required of Mary. God invited her to become a mother in a manner that was contrary to all the laws of nature. Preposterous to the mundane mind, but faith says "nothing is impossible with God."

Her divine maternity demanded an even greater risk. In those days an illegitimate pregnancy was punishable by death. How could she conceivably survive to bring her child to viable maturity? Only a total commitment in faith could hold the answer. And that faith was rewarded.   **David E. Rosage**

But above all, in the Church of that time and of every time, Mary was and is the one who is "blessed because she believed"; *she was the first to believe.* From the moment of the Annunciation and conception, from the moment of his birth in the stable at Bethlehem, Mary followed Jesus step by step in her maternal pilgrimage of faith. She followed him during the years of his hidden life at Nazareth; she followed him also during the time after he left home, when he began "to do and to teach" (cf Acts 1:1) in the midst of Israel. Above all she followed him in the tragic experience of Golgotha.

Pope John Paul II, *Redemptoris Mater*

Perhaps the physical revelation or presence of Jesus often tested Mary's faith in ways that ours shall never be. From the beginning of her life with Jesus, she had known thrilling mountaintops and also deep valleys. Like the colorful arc of a rainbow, certain events stand out with appealing interest. But between and during those peak moments was the continual demand to walk steadily on by faith.

Mary's faith would be stretched incredibly in the coming events, but she would be richer for each experience. Her life had to fade softly into the background as the child who played at her feet grew, for He would draw people of all nations to Himself.

June Miller

We do well to envisage the family at Nazareth as people engaged in a struggle for their faith, bravely facing all life's difficulties in their complete surrender to God's supreme rule. The true and complete picture of Mary's life is not to be found in the apocrypha of the New Testament, but in the sober account of the Gospels.

Her life does not follow the pattern of a fairy tale, like that of Snow White. No little forest birds hold her clothes in their beaks and carry her away out of reach of danger to the accompaniment of sweet, heavenly music. If this were so, she would not be an example of strength for us in our day-to-day struggle with the harsh realities of a life which is anything but a fairy tale. She would simply be a narcotic, and we should wake up after the effects had worn off to face the stern reality of life with a feeling of inconsolable dreariness even more powerful than before.

Mary's life was, like ours, truly human, and she was also involved in the same sort of oppressive, hopeless and often apparently insoluble social situations in which every human being is at some time or another placed. But she showed us, by her example, how faith in the mystery of the living God is stronger than human life, stronger, too, than death—even the death of her own Messiah. **Edward Schillebeeckx, O.P.**

Mary is the great believer who humbly offered herself to God as an empty vessel for him to use in his mysterious plan. Without complaint she surrendered control of her life; she did not try to live according to human calculation but put herself completely at the disposal of God's mysterious, incomprehensible design. All she wanted to be was the handmaid of the Lord, the instrument and servant of the Word. Therein lies her true fame: that she remained a believer despite all the darkness and all the inexplicable demands God made on her.

Cardinal Joseph Ratzinger

But Mary kept all these things, pondering them in her heart. **Luke 2:19**

Mary, you were a perfect listener. You pondered in your heart every word spoken concerning Jesus. You listened to every event in his life. You attended to every action in which he expressed what was in him. You heard every word in which he manifested his heart.

When you did not understand the words he spoke to you (Luke 2:50), you did not dismiss them with an indifferent shrug. Rather, you "kept all these things in [your] heart" (Luke 2:51), pondering them until you did understand. Love ever seeks understanding, and seeks till it finds.   **Paul Hinnebusch, O.P.**

Pondering or keeping in the heart is not a locking away or hiding process, although often those things which are most profound sink and grow within us and are not taken out and shared until later, much later, when they have reached maturity. Pondering in the heart is a prayer-reflection process leading to light and wisdom.

Mary can be a model in handling the impossible in our lives, which will parallel hers. We won't meet Simeon in the temple, but we may listen to a doctor's report: "Your child has a serious disease. By the age of sixteen he will be…" At the awareness of death or suffering for self or a loved one, we can scream in agony, weep in rage, demand of God, "Why?" We can also remember Mary and ask her to teach us. "What do I do with this? How could anyone bear this?"

The message may be clear enough but the real message, God's plan in all this agony, is not clear. To bring light to the confusion and peace to the chaos in our hearts we need to pray, to reflect. Mary learned that and she can help us, if we are willing to accept that help.   **John Randall, S.T.D.**

In a new and deeper way the mother Mary had to learn to keep faith and wait patiently for God's timing. At first she would have waited from one year to the next, and then, when Jesus entered manhood, from month to month, week to week, and finally from day to day, for the moment when at last He would disclose His identity and when the angel's prophecy at the annunciation of His birth would be fulfilled. Would God now give Him the throne of His father David? Would He be proclaimed King of Israel and enter upon His God-given office?

Basilea Schlink

This Mary had never foreseen—that the throne of his father David would consist of two rough pieces of wood. And what of the kingdom without end? The Nazareth prophecies and the events on Golgotha were, humanly speaking, too far apart to be reconciled.

Mary knew it; but she saw the Nazareth scene, and what was now happening outside Jerusalem, with the eyes of faith. The faith of Nazareth had grown greater and richer in the course of many years; the power of grace granted her then had never deserted Mary; from this grace, and from that precious moment when it was bestowed—a moment which, now, at the foot of the cross, appeared drained of all meaning—there yet brimmed to the surface of her overflowing heart her *fiat* of yore: "Behold the Lord's slave. Let it be unto me according to thy word."

Josef Weiger

Mary, your example of purity,
faith, and humble obedience
inspires me to be a better disciple.
Pray for me in the midst of difficulties,
that I may always follow your Son, Jesus,
and love God with all my heart.
Through Christ our Lord. Amen.

Obedient and Willing

But years, or ages, or eternity,
    Will find me still in thought before your throne,
Pondering the mystery of Maternity,
    Soul within Soul—Mother and Child in One!

Help me to see! not with my mimic sight—
    With yours! which carried radiance, like the sun,
Giving the rays you saw with—light in light—
    Tying all suns and stars and world in one.

Help me to know! not with my mocking art—
    With you, who knew yourself unbound by laws;

Gave God your strength, your life, your sight, your
  heart,
    And took from him the Thought that Is—
      the Cause.

Help me to feel! not with my insect sense—
    With yours that felt all life alive in you;
Infinite heart beating at your expense;
    Infinite passion breathing the breath you drew!

"Prayer to the Dynamo"
by Henry Adams

*Mary's fiat exemplifies obedience as well as faith.
Indeed, she consistently demonstrated her faith by an obe-
dient and willing spirit, by her works as well as her words.
Mary believed God's word and acted on it.*

The knot tied by Eve's disobedience was untied by
the obedience of Mary. **St. Irenaeus**

Because Mary was free from original sin, she found
no obstacle in obeying God; she was like a wheel,
which was easily turned by every inspiration of the
Holy Ghost. **St. Bonaventure**

As he said this, a woman in the crowd raised her
voice and said to him, "Blessed is the womb that
bore you, and the breasts that you sucked!" But he
said, "Blessed rather are those who hear the word of
God and keep it!" **Luke 11:27-28**

Mary is blest because she hears the Word of God and she obeys. Jesus loves and admires his mother not only because she was his mother, but also because that was God's plan for her and she accepted it. Jesus invites all to be blest. Certainly only one could be his mother. It is equally certain, however, that all could keep the Word of the Father—all could be blest. The word "blest" is sometimes translated "happy." Jesus publicly announces that anyone who wants it can have true happiness. The key to it is hearing and doing the will of the Father. Mary had the key, and she used it.   John Randall, S.T.D.

Our Lady, knowing God as she did, knew that his law is the voice of love. It is not a litany of "thou shalt not," but the vigilance of infinite love. Moreover, our Lady kept and loved the law not for herself alone, but for all the mothers of Christ yet to be, for all the unborn Christ-children who would need it for sword, and for shield, and for cloak.

The law is the hands of God cupped round the flame of life, tending it in the driving storm.

Caryll Houselander

But the sacred Virgin voluntarily subjected herself to the law of purification because she loved the commandment, and the thing commanded was so precious to her. Although she was not obliged to it, she did not hesitate to fulfill it because of the love she had for obedience and for God who had given this commandment. But, O most holy Lady, you have no need for it. "It is true," she replies: "but other women, for whom I should serve as an example, need it; I obey this law as much for the profit of those who are found by it as because of the love I bear it."

St. Francis de Sales

We should do wrong to attribute to Mary a kind of omniscience or a striking activity. Her greatness lies singly and solely in her pure receptivity. She is not in competition with the sovereignty of God, but is the person who acknowledged this sovereignty in the most radical fashion. She is the greatest of the faithful, always wondering about her Son, and following him to the foot of the cross.   **Ansfried Hulsbosch**

Mary and Joseph, both of the Davidic line, went to Bethlehem to be enrolled in accordance with the edict of the emperor Augustus.... The holy pair did not reflect that in issuing his order the emperor was motivated by ambition and self-interest. No: they learned of the command and immediately obeyed.... Mary obeyed like everyone else, and better than everyone else, because she obeyed humbly, patiently, and without murmuring.

She saw in the emperor's order the will of God. The order was, in her eyes, an act of Divine Providence and she submitted without questioning.

Obedience does not argue; simplicity is its hallmark. There is nothing more opposed to the spirit of submissiveness than the worldly prudence that wants to see and examine everything.

Alexander de Rouville

Though she drank to the dregs her cup of sorrow, she never faltered. Though she often pondered, she never questioned. Though she did not always understand, she never doubted. Though at times she was set aside, she never rebelled.   **Mother Angelica**

> *Mary, your example of purity,*
> *faith, and humble obedience*
> *inspires me to be a better disciple.*
> *Pray for me in the midst of difficulties,*
> *that I may always follow your Son, Jesus,*
> *and love God with all my heart.*
> *Through Christ our Lord. Amen.*

Embracing Sorrows and Hardships

They warned Our Lady for the Child
   That was Our blessed Lord,
And She took Him into the desert wild,
   Over the camel's ford.

And a long song She sang to Him
   And a short story told.
And She wrapped Him in a woollen cloak
   To keep Him from the cold.

But when Our Lord was grown a man
   The Rich they dragged Him down,
And they crucified Him in Golgotha,
   Out and beyond the Town.

They crucified Him on Calvary,
    Upon an April day;
And because He had been her little Son
    She followed Him all the way.

Our Lady stood beside the Cross,
    A little space apart,
And when She heard Our Lord cry out
    A sword went through Her heart.

> **"Our Lord and Our Lady"**
> **by Hilaire Belloc**

Mary proved herself to be faithful and obedient even in the midst of sorrows and hardships. Like any disciple who walks the way of Christ, she learned obedience through what she suffered (Hebrews 5:8). We can learn much from Mary to help us to embrace suffering in our own lives.

Nazareth was a small place and did not have a good reputation. There were probably many malicious tongues in the town. How Mary must have suffered from them! What contemptuous looks and insults she would have borne when she but left her home to draw water or go about her daily chores! We have little idea how hard it must have been for Mary, because our laws do not impose the death penalty on a woman for having an illegitimate child.

Appearances were against Mary, and since by law she would incur such severe punishment, Joseph wanted to dismiss her quietly, so that he would not have to report her. Nonetheless, this was no guarantee that her countrymen would not take her to court and punish her. What agonies Mary must have endured during those months! **Basilea Schlink**

With this long and strenuous journey to Bethlehem, the Lord placed upon Mary and, no doubt, Joseph, a new burden, for what a strain it must have been travelling for days across the mountains in that condition! Could not the Lord have made it easier for her, seeing that He was the Father of the Son that she would give birth to? Was He not the almighty God, Maker and Ruler of the whole world, with all things at His disposal? But it was God's plan for Mary that she should follow this path of poverty and physical strain, where her soul was afflicted with cares, fears, and many anxious questions: "What if the Child is born on the way?" and: "Where shall I take shelter? Where shall I find lodging?" **Basilea Schlink**

Mary lived a life of poverty and suffering even though she was close to Jesus, Who could have made her wealthy and happy on this earth by a single act of His will. But she never asked her divine Son for worldly happiness. She regarded Jesus as her only treasure and her happiness consisted in perfect obedience to the will of God. When she arrived in Bethlehem with her holy spouse, St. Joseph, she could not find room in the inn or any of the houses. This did not matter to her. She found refuge in a sta-

ble and there she gave birth to Jesus, the only treasure of her life.   **Cardinal Antonio Bacci**

During her life on this earth Mary surrendered un-
conditionally to the living God whenever she found
herself in difficulty. This should always be an
encouragement to us. We are too readily inclined to
believe, simply because we are Christians, go to
church on Sundays, and fulfill our Christian duties,
that everything in our lives is bound to be plain sail-
ing—that we should, as a matter of course, never
encounter any real adversity, especially in our family
lives.   **Edward Schillebeeckx, O.P.**

Seven sorrows of Mary—Seven Sorrows there were,
which stabbed the heart of Mary! Other painful and
anxious moments could no doubt be listed, but these
seven could be experienced by no other human... for
Mary was the Mother of God and her sorrow was
inflicted on her by what the sins of man would do to
her Son: Simeon's prophecy; the flight into Egypt; the
loss in the temple; meeting Jesus on the way to
Calvary; the crucifixion of Jesus; his removal from
the cross; and the burial of Jesus.

There was no selfish sorrow in Mary. She could
think only of her Son. It was the events in Christ's
life, her Son, her flesh and blood, that caused her
pain... and this only because she willed to be a part
of her Son in His Redemptive life.
Day by Day With My Daily Visitor

And what inner conflict Mary must have endured at the mere thought that all those infants in Bethlehem would be slaughtered by Herod's soldiers for the sake of her Child! Oh, what anguish that must have caused her! How could she still understand God? But she went on following His leadings in obedience and, though not being able to understand Him, kept on trusting Him in the assurance that the ways of the Lord are good. All she could do was endure the pain and anguish of soul, but in so doing embrace and kiss the Babe ever anew, as we sing in a German Christmas carol:

> Whoever yearns to hold this Child
> And kiss Him joyfully
> Has first to suffer with Him
> Much pain and agony.　　**Basilea Schlink**

I now saw the Holy Family on Egyptian territory. They were in flat country, with green pastures here and there on which cattle were feeding. I saw trees to which idols had been fastened in the shape of infants wrapped in broad swaddling-bands inscribed with figures or letters. Here and there I saw people thick-set and fat, dressed like the cotton-spinners whom I once saw near the frontiers of the three kings. I saw these people hurrying to worship their idols.

The Holy Family went into a shed; there were beasts in it, but these went out to make room for them. Their provisions had given out, and they had

neither bread nor water. Nobody gave them anything, and Mary was hardly able to feed her Child.
They did, indeed, endure every human misery.

Anne Catherine Emmerich

She had fled with that child away into a foreign land,
with bloodshed in her wake; almost from the first the
joy of motherhood had been marred by this agony.
Her own child's life had brought death to many children, desolation to many mothers. She had brought
him back from exile in fear and trembling, longing to
live in Bethlehem, the home of David, but they dared
not; hiding at last in Nazareth, the village of no
repute, lest evil men might again discover him and
seek his life.   **Alban Goodier**

Since the fall of Eve, God in His love is obliged to
lead us through many trials and sorrows if He is to
achieve His objective with us. But with Mary even
more was involved. She was to give birth to the Man
of Sorrows, who was destined to tread the path of
sorrows for our sakes. As mother of our Lord would
she not share His path? Thus she was called to a life
of disgrace, scorn, loneliness, humiliation, poverty,
and homelessness.   **Basilea Schlink**

As each evening drew near, My heart would be
crushed with this painful memory: "One day less to
wait, one day less before Calvary." This would drown

My soul with sorrow, as if a wave of torments had washed over it. This was a preview of the tide that would engulf Me on Golgotha. I would lean My spirit on that happy memory [of Jesus's birth] which had remained alive in My heart, as someone bends over a mountain gorge to hear again the echo of a love song, and to see his beloved's house in the distance.

Maria Valtorta's untranslated Notebooks of 1943

Every woman who sees her child, every woman who is separated from her child, every woman who must stand by helpless and see her child die, every woman who echoes the old cry, "Why, why, why my child?" has the answer from the Mother of Christ. She can look at the child through Mary's eyes, she can know the answer with Mary's mind, she can accept the suffering with Mary's will, she can love Christ in her child with Mary's heart—because Mary has made her a mother of Christ. It is Christ who suffers in her child; it is his innocence redeeming the world, his love saving the world. He too is about his Father's business, the business of love. **Caryll Houselander**

> *Mary, your example of purity,*
> *faith, and humble obedience*
> *inspires me to be a better disciple.*
> *Pray for me in the midst of difficulties,*
> *that I may always follow your Son, Jesus,*
> *and love God with all my heart.*
> *Through Christ our Lord. Amen.*

The Death of a Son

At the cross her station keeping
Stood the mournful Mother weeping,
    Close to Jesus to the last;
Through her heart, His sorrow sharing,
All His bitter anguish bearing,
    Now at length the sword had passed.
O how sad and sore distressed
Was that Mother highly blest
    Of the sole-begotten One!
Christ above in torment hangs.
She beneath beholds the pangs
    Of her dying glorious Son.
Is there one who would not weep
Whelmed in miseries so deep
    Christ's dear Mother to behold?
Can the human heart refrain
From partaking in her pain,
    in that Mother's pain untold?
Bruised, derided, cursed, defiled,
She beheld her tender Child
    All with bloody scourges rent;
For the sake of His own nation,
Saw Him hang in desolation,
    Till His spirit forth He sent.
O thou Mother, fount of love,
Touch my spirit from above,
    Make my heart with thine accord!
Make me feel as thou hast felt;

Make my soul to glow and melt
With the love of Christ my Lord. **"Stabat Mater Dolorosa"**
by Jacopone da Todi

*Mary endured her greatest grief at the foot of the cross
as she watched her Son suffer a horrible death. How did
she bear the pain? How could she not cry out in protest?
Let us learn from Mary how to be at the foot of the cross in
our own lives. Let us remember that she is ever there with
us—making it lighter, making it sweeter.*

*Mary also wept at the tomb. Burying her child must be
one of the most difficult tasks of any mother, and Mary
was burying not only her Son, but the Son of God. With
the anguish of a mother, she cried out, "How can I bury
you, my Son?" Only by the grace of God. Only for the
love of God. Even in her deepest grief, Mary proves the
model disciple.*

Her child, from the time he was arrested until the
time he died, was covered with bruises, cuts, sores,
wounds, and welts. He was humiliated in every way.
He was spat upon and degraded. Mary followed him
along the way of the cross, and she felt his pain. Her
heart, as Simeon prophesied, was pierced. *Mater
Dolorosa*, Mother of Sorrows.

She watched him tortured, spilling his blood in
the gutters of Jerusalem. And she accepted it all.
"Father, may your will be done in this." If she had
not agreed to this crucifixion, she would have died

on the road to Calvary. She could not have survived seeing the Son of the Most High tormented so.

Mary did agree because she had spent fifty years learning that "Blessed is he who does the will of my Father." She agreed. At the moment she said yes to the way of the cross, yes to the falling and spitting and beating, at the moment she said, "Father, may your will be done—I accept this horror," at that moment Mary became the mother of mankind. She agreed to the redemption. She gave her Son. She let him go, carrying his cross, and she accepted the Father's plan. Mary, the mother of the Redeemer, became the mother of the redeemed. She became the mother of all mankind.   **John Randall, S.T.D.**

Those wounds which were scattered over the body of our Lord were all united in the single heart of Mary. **St. Bonaventure**

The procession reached the hill of Golgotha. Her Son was deprived of His clothes and stood naked before all the people. Then He was laid on the wooden beam of the cross, and the terrible moment came for the mother Mary when she heard the hammer blows as the huge nails were driven into His flesh. In former times she had often heard the sound of hammering in her house when Joseph and Jesus too drove nails into wood. But this time—oh, how incomprehensible it must have been for her!—the hammer pounded on nails piercing the hands and feet of her own Son.   **Basilea Schlink**

Now there stood by the cross of Jesus His Mother (John 19:25). Whereas other martyrs sacrifice their own lives, the Blessed Virgin consummated her martyr-dom by sacrificing the life of her Son, a life which she loved far more than her own, and which exceeded all other torments ever endured by any mortal on earth.   **St. Antoninus**

The Gospel records as a matter of course that Mary stood at the foot of the Cross on Calvary. She was there in the thick of the mob, whereas the apostles had fled, for she had to unite her compassion with the redemptive Passion. Her faith penetrated every veil, every outrage, every wound; her whole soul was united, trembling yet clear-sighted, with the mystery of salvation, enacted before her. Her part therein, was to give mankind's consent and she did not refuse it.   **Cardinal Léon Joseph Suenens**

But Mary, this is not Bethlehem; this is Calvary. He is not white as He came from the Father, but red as He came from us. In the crib He was as a chalice of the offertory, full of the red wine of life. Now, at the foot of the Cross, His Body is as a chalice drained of the drops of blood for the redemption of mankind. There was no room in the inn at His Birth; there is no room in the inn for His death. "The Son of Man hath nowhere to lay His Head"—except in the arms of His Mother.   **Fulton J. Sheen**

A grown-up son is still his mother's boy—however mature he may be, he never ceases, as far as she is concerned, to be "a child." How can we, then, imagine Mary's human agony when her Child met her on the way to Calvary and later, when she saw him, her divine Child, die on the Cross? And what human suffering did she not experience when finally she took the dead Jesus on her lap and clasped his body to her breast—she whose womb had been the witness of a mystery which heralded the salvation and redemption of the world?

... She will take the racked treasure of our suffering on her knees and place it beside the tortured relic of Christ's body. Her lap contains all the suffering of the whole of humanity, the countless, ever-growing number of wounds of a human race which is continuously crucified. She is the great *Pietà* who casts her mother's cloak of mercy over our suffering humanity. She is the living womb in which, as in a second act of bodily motherhood, we are carried for the nine long months of our lives until we at last come to the glory of redemption and resurrection.

Edward Schillebeeckx, O.P.

"Thus bitter death doth part"; and once more Mary held her Child upon her lap, her arms around him, covering his brow with her kisses, with streaming tears beholding the searing marks which devils in human form had inflicted on his most sacred face. Again and again throughout Christian times artists have tried their hand at depicting this scene: Mary with her Son's dead body. So Jesus' life ended, as it had begun in Bethlehem, in his mother's arms for all the world to see—in his mother's arms once more.

Josef Weiger

At that moment, when Our Lady received the love of the Holy Spirit as the wedded love of her soul, she also received her dead son in her arms. The trust which accepted the utter sweetness of the Infant Jesus between her own hands, looking at her with her own eyes, accepted the stiff, unresponsive corpse that her hands embalmed. This was her son, but more, even more, God's Son. She trusted God, she understood on earth that which many mothers will understand only in heaven; she was able to see her boy killed, lying there bruised from head to foot, wounded and dead, and to believe the Father's cry: "This is my beloved Son, in whom I am well pleased." **Caryll Houselander**

All the fatherless, motherless, sonless, husbandless, and wifeless griefs, that ever tore at the hearts of human beings, were now bearing down on the soul of Mary. The most any human being ever lost in a bereavement was a creature, but Mary was burying the Son of God. It is hard to lose a son or a daughter, but it is harder to bury Christ. To be motherless is a tragedy, but to be Christless is hell. **Fulton J. Sheen**

Though it would seem that nothing could be added to the Blessed Virgin's afflicted state, yet her sorrowful heart still received from time to time fresh wounds resulting from different circumstances of her Son's passion. Such circumstances were when she heard him cry out: *My God, my God, why have you forsaken me?* When she saw him offered gall and vinegar to quench the burning thirst of which he complained. When he sent forth that loud cry when he expired. When she received him dead in her arms after he had been taken down from the cross. When he was buried; and when she saw herself deprived of the presence of her loved One whose resurrection she desired so ardently that those three days seemed to her like three years. **Venerable Thomas of Jesus**

> *Mary, your example of purity,*
> *faith, and humble obedience*
> *inspires me to be a better disciple.*
> *Pray for me in the midst of difficulties,*
> *that I may always follow your Son, Jesus,*
> *and love God with all my heart.*
> *Through Christ our Lord. Amen.*

Loving God above All

Mary was a meadow for the Lord
Mary was his rich and fertile plain
Mary was the planted field, Jesus was the seed,
Jesus is the harvest yield
to fill our every need—
Mary, make my life a fertile plain
reap in me your rare and golden grain.

Mary was a crystal for the Lord
Mary was the prism of his light
Mary was the windowed wall, Jesus was the ray,
Jesus is the rainbow fall
to cheer our every day—
Mary be my crystal for the light
hold him ever glowing in my sight.

Mary was a woodwind for the Lord
Mary was his pure and tranquil tone
Mary was the perfect key, Jesus was the song,
Jesus is the melody for all to sing along—
Mary make my love a perfect tone
that my heart may sing for God alone.

"Mary Was a Meadow"
by Bill Peffley

*Mary had surely faced the ultimate test of her faith and
love of God. Just as Abraham had been asked to sacrifice
his only son, Mary had been asked to sacrifice Jesus. But*

this time, God did not provide a sacrificial lamb at the last minute—for Jesus himself was the spotless Lamb of God slain for us all. Truly God could say to Mary, "Now I know that you fear God, seeing you have not withheld your son, your only son, from me" (Genesis 22:12).

The love of God had so deeply wounded and penetrated the Heart of Mary, that there was nothing left in it that was not filled with love; for God inflamed no other heart with His love so much as that of the Blessed Virgin. For as she was free from all attachment to earthly things, so she was most susceptible to the flames of this blessed fire.   **St. Bernard**

With her Yes, she gave herself unreservedly to God, expressing her readiness to be the handmaid and bondservant of the Lord for Him to do with as He pleased and as He had said. A Yes like this can be uttered only by a person whose desires and wishes are completely one with the will of God. This was the Yes of love. A soul that loves God cannot bear to refuse Him any wish or decline any proposal of His. It was the Yes expressive of a readiness to die. She did not flinch at burying her reputation, her hopes for the future, a happy marriage, or at the prospect of losing her home and all security. She committed herself to a way of life that would mean daily dying to self and to all personal happiness in this world.

Basilea Schlink

Mary is made for God alone. Far from keeping any soul in herself, she casts each one upon God. And the more perfectly a soul is united to her, the more perfectly does she unite it to her Father, her Spouse [the Holy Spirit], and her Son.

Mary is the wonderful echo of God. When we say "Mary," she answers, "God." When, with St. Elizabeth we call her "Blessed," she magnifies the Lord.

St. Louis de Montfort

The Magnificat is Our Lady's prayer of thanks. She can help us to love Jesus best; she is the one who can show us the shortest way to Jesus. Mary was the one whose intercession led Jesus to work the first miracle. "They have no wine," she said to Jesus. "Do whatever he tells you," she said to the servants. We take the part of the servants. Let us go to her with great love and trust. We are serving Jesus in the distressing disguise of the poor.   **Mother Teresa of Calcutta**

Mary is preeminently faithful to her Lord and Son. Let no one for an instant suppose that she is not supremely zealous for His honor, or as those who are not Catholics fancy, that to exalt her is to be unfaithful to Him. Her true servants are still more truly His. Well as she rewards her friends, she would deem him no friend, but a traitor, who preferred her to Him. As He is zealous for her honor, so is she for His. He is the Fount of grace, and all her gifts are from His goodness.   **Cardinal John Henry Newman**

Always and everywhere, Mary is "Our Lady of Advent": she who predisposes us, opens our hearts, strengthens our weakness, and overcomes our resistance. It is her special function to free us from all that is opposed to God's action in us. She detaches us from ourselves, purifies us, and unburdens us so as to prepare ample room in us for our Lord. For such, in fine, is her whole office. I unite myself to her, and to her influence, now in order that Christ may grow in me.   **Cardinal Léon Joseph Suenens**

She is God's instrument. With full consciousness and total willingness she allows God to govern her; she consents to his will, desires only what he desires, and acts according to his will in the most perfect manner, without failing, without ever turning aside from his will. She makes perfect use of the powers and privileges God has given her, so as to fulfill always and in everything whatever God wants of her, purely for love of God, One and Three.   **St. Maximilian Kolbe**

The Blessed Virgin does not disillusion any of the profound expectations of the men and women of our time but offers them the perfect model of the disciple of the Lord: the disciple who builds up the earthly and temporal city while being a diligent pilgrim towards the heavenly and eternal city; the disciple who works for that justice which sets free the oppressed and for that charity which assists the needy; but above all, the disciple who is the active witness of that love which builds up Christ in people's hearts.   **Pope Paul VI**

From the moment that she had the use of reason, that is, from the first moment of her immaculate conception in the womb of St. Anne, she began to love God with all her strength, and continued to do so, always advancing more and more throughout her whole life in love and perfection. And all her thoughts, desires, and affections were of and for God alone; she never uttered a word, made a movement, cast a glance, or breathed, but for God and his glory; and never departed a step or detached herself for a single moment from the divine love.   **St. Alphonsus**

I have seen many creatures worship their Saviour Jesus after being healed or converted by Him. None of them, however, adores Him in remotely the same way as Mary does. Even the most passionate among them fail to worship as well as Mary does. The same is true of those who are so moved by love that they do not realize that their gestures are exaggerated. As for Mary, I dare say that *Her love is… greater than that of any other creature.*

Oh! She is really God's faultless Daughter! That is why She can love Him so well…. This reminds me of what mankind lost because of original sin…. It reminds me of what Satan robbed us when he led our first parents astray. He took away from us the capacity to love God as Mary loved Him.... Satan took away from us the capacity to love well.

Maria Valtorta, *The Poem of the Man-God, vol. 4*

Heaven was the cell of the heavenly and most Blessed Virgin Mary; for, being there with all her desires and affections, she made it her continual abode. Her school was eternity; for she was always detached and free from temporal possessions. Her teacher was divine truth; for her whole life was guided by this alone. Her book was the purity of her own conscience, in which she always found occasion to rejoice in the Lord. Her mirror was the divinity; for she never admitted any representations into her soul but such as were transformed into and clothed with God, so that she might always conform herself to his will. Her ornament was devotion; for she attended solely to her interior sanctification, and was always ready to fulfill the divine commands. Her repose was union with God; for he alone was her treasure and the resting-place of her soul.   **Johann Tauler**

Mary, your example of purity,
faith, and humble obedience

inspires me to be a better disciple.
Pray for me in the midst of difficulties,
that I may always follow your Son, Jesus,
and love God with all my heart.
Through Christ our Lord. Amen.

THREE

The Model of Womanhood

In the midst of controversy concerning women's rights and women's liberation, the essence of womanhood easily becomes clouded. Because the media so often focuses on nearly impossible standards of physical beauty, many women suffer low self-esteem. What is true womanly beauty? What characterizes the perfect woman?

Mary of Nazareth was a simple country girl, a poor woman, a carpenter's wife. She never wrote a book or painted a picture, never traveled very far from the obscure village where she was born. Yet no woman has ever inspired more authors or artists than has Mary, the mother of Jesus. What was it in Mary's life that evokes such love and praise?

In Mary, God has given us an example of a woman who is gentle yet strong, humble yet bold, hidden yet active. Mary is a woman who gives her all to God in complete faith and trust, yet one who takes profound risks in obeying God's call. Mary exulted in being the handmaid of the Lord. Is she not the model of true liberation?

The Perfect Woman

Seraph of heaven! too gentle to be human,
Veiling beneath that radiant form of Woman
All that is insupportable in thee
Of light, and love, and immortality!
Sweet Benediction in the eternal Curse!
Veiled glory of this lampless Universe!
Thou Moon beyond the clouds! Thou living Form
Among the Dead! Thou Star above the Storm!
Thou Wonder, and thou Beauty, and thou Terror!
Thou Harmony of Nature's art! Thou Mirror
In whom, as in the splendour of the Sun,
All shapes look glorious which thou gazest on!
Ay, even the dim words which obscure thee now
Flash, lightning-like, with unaccustomed glow;
I pray thee that thou blot from this sad song
All of its much mortality and wrong,
With those clear drops, which start like sacred dew
From the twin lights thy sweet soul darkens through,

Weeping, till sorrow becomes ecstasy:
Then smile on it, so that it may not die.
"Seraph of Heaven"
by Percy Bysshe Shelley

We may complain at times that God has told us so little about her, about her appearance, her personality, her words and deeds. In so complaining, we miss the point. God has told us what we need to know. He has included in Mary's vocation and in her life's work the one essential thing that lies hidden and must be revealed in every vocation and in every life's work: to bear Christ in our hearts and carry His light to the world. This Mary did while remaining lowly and obscure, a lay woman among the people of her village, doing the ordinary daily tasks of her home, just being what God wanted her to be.

Leo A. Pursley, D.D.

Like a child digging for buried treasure I have explored the life of Mary, the mother of our Lord Jesus Christ. The search has been rewarded with amazing, practical solutions for my life today. The issues that confronted Mary as a woman, wife, and mother present a master pattern by which we can discover a meaningful future filled with the happiness we are afraid to hope for. When the fabric of our lives is silhouetted against the situation she faced, we find more exciting and valuable help than can be gained from any current group-therapy or psychology class.

June Miller

In Mary we find the essence of womanhood so con-
centrated that the light of the ideal flows down from
her to invest every woman with something of its
splendor. That is no mere figure of speech, and it is
besides, a fact to which history itself bears witness. In
Mary's perfection, by a certain communication of
privilege, the women of Christendom shared; she
found a place she never occupied before Christ came
to give her true emancipation.   Father James, O.F.M. Cap.

Woman is not, by nature of grace, the mere echo of
man. She is truly free only when she is free to be herself, to develop in herself those qualities that make
her more womanly. She is not emancipated when she
is granted the dubious privilege of being less womanly. Whether she is destined for marriage or not, she
is always a mother at heart; she is always a fountain
of life, not only in a physical sense but in a moral and
spiritual sense. That is why she cannot renounce her
motherhood, even in this larger comprehension,
without denying to God and man her unique contri-
bution to the glory of the One and the good of the
other.

And that is why we pray that Mary, the woman
who comforts, the Mother who gives strength to
troubled minds and weak wills and timid hearts and
tired hands, Mary, the Seat of Wisdom, may intercede for all women that they may know their own
worth, their place in God's plan, the glory of their
vocation; that they may take the wounded world

into their arms, even as Mary clasped the lifeless
body of her Son; that they may hasten with the holy
women to the empty tomb and lead us out of darkness and death into the newborn life of the risen
Christ.   **Leo A. Pursley, D.D.**

To extol the gift of grace and to humiliate human
wisdom, God chose to take flesh from a woman, a
virgin, to restore like to like, to cure contrary by contrary, to pluck out the painful thorn, to delete the
handwriting of sin.

Eve was a thorn, but Mary was a rose. Eve, the
thorn, inflicted wounds, but Mary, the rose, soothed
all passions. Eve, the thorn, brought death, but Mary,
the rose, made salvation accessible.

Mary, the rose, had the glowing whiteness of virginity, the brilliant red of charity. She had purity of
body, beauty of soul. The whiteness signifies her pur-
suit of virtue, her purity of mind, her great love of
God. The redness manifests her triumph over vice,
her mortification of the flesh, her compassion for her
neighbor.   **St. Bernard**

The Virgin Mary has a human mind filled with
divine light, and a human heart overflowing with
divine love. Wherever She goes, whatever She does,
She brings a whiff of heavenly perfume: that of Her
eminent virtues.... While apparently like all other
women, She is actually a miracle of physical and
moral beauty. She is a Woman Who walks on the

earth with Her spirit and heart always centered on Heaven. A prodigious Woman. A Woman of paradise, even while still of the earth; a perpetual delight, support and comfort for Her divine Son.

Gabriel M. Roschini, O.S.M.

The perfection of Mary's womanhood stands out most sharply in the supreme moments of her life: in her divine maternity and her preparation for it.... Mary's perfection is brought out from the confused detail of her age by the application of these basic tests of any woman's life: sanctity, virginity, marriage, the evaluation of the infant. Mary, seen from the vantage of these basic tests, leaves no room for doubt of the basis upon which woman's life is lived to its fullest.

It must, of course, be remembered that Mary is a model in the order of nature as well as in the order of grace. Grace does not destroy but rather perfects nature. Mary, then, is the exemplar for women, not only in so far as she is the holiest of women, but also as the most womanly of women, the most free, winning the highest possible place in the hearts and minds of men. **F. J. Sheed**

The modern woman will note with pleasant surprise that Mary of Nazareth, while completely devoted to the will of God, was far from being a timidly submissive woman or one whose piety was repellent to others; on the contrary, she was a woman who did not hesitate to proclaim that God vindicates the humble and the oppressed, and removes the powerful people of this world from their privileged positions (cf. Luke 1:51-53). The modern woman will recognize in Mary, who "stands out among the poor and humble of the Lord," a woman of strength, who experienced poverty and suffering, flight and exile. **Pope Paul VI**

Christianity does not ask the modern woman to be exclusively a Martha or a Mary; the choice is not between a professional career and contemplation, for the Church reads the Gospel of Martha and Mary for Our Lady to symbolize that she combines both the speculative and the practical, the serving of the Lord and the sitting at His Feet.

If woman wants to be a revolutionist, then *The Woman* is her guide, for she sang the most revolutionary song ever written—the *Magnificat,* the burden of which was the abolition of principalities and powers, and the exaltation of the humble. She breaks the shell of woman's isolation from the world and puts woman back into the wide ocean of humanity. She, who is the Cosmopolitan Woman, gives us the Cosmopolitan Man, for which giving all generations shall call her blessed. **Fulton J. Sheen**

Hers was the hidden treasure of modesty, hers the self sacrifice of earnestness, hers to be the pattern of maidenhood at home, of kinswomanhood in ministry, of motherhood in the temple. **St. Ambrose**

The most remarkable thing about Mary is that such an extraordinary woman would live such an ordinary life. It was her humility that made her appear as any other woman, so much so that many throughout the centuries have refused to acknowledge God's gifts in her—as if these gifts came from herself or she did not possess them. We deprive God of glory if we do not look at the Promised Woman and praise His Power for what it has wrought in her. It is like a king who carves an image of himself in a large diamond and gives it to us to behold, but we refuse and throw it away because we think it is only glass.

Mother Angelica

Mary most holy, Mother of God, passes unnoticed, as just one more among the women of her town. Learn from her how to live with "naturalness."

Josemaria Escriva de Balaguer

The figure of Mary of Nazareth sheds light on *womanhood as such* by the very fact that God, in the sublime event of the Incarnation of his Son, entrusted himself to the ministry, the free and active ministry of a woman. It can thus be said that women, by looking to Mary, find in her the secret of living their femininity with dignity and of achieving their own true advancement.

In the light of Mary, the Church sees in the face of women the reflection of a beauty which mirrors the loftiest sentiments of which the human heart is capable: the self-offering totality of love; the strength that is capable of bearing the greatest sorrows; limitless fidelity and tireless devotion to work; the ability to combine penetrating intuition with words of support and encouragement. **Pope John Paul II,** *Mater Redemptoris*

And when they met her they all blessed her with one accord and said to her, "You are the exaltation of Jerusalem, you are the great glory of Israel, you are the great pride of our nation! You have done all this singlehanded; you have done great good to Israel, and God is well pleased with it. May the Almighty Lord bless you for ever!" And all the people said, "So be it!" **Judith 15:9-10**

Right in the center of this universal scenario of misery there is raised up an exceptional and ideal figure, unsullied and unblemished, the object of God's overwhelming love: the Lord is with you, Mary; you are the chosen one, the blessed among all women, excelling in goodness, beauty and immaculate purity, a woman unique and full of grace, the incomparable model of virgin and mother, chosen to offer stainless flesh to the Word of God, who in you Mary, becomes our Brother, Teacher, and Savior. **Pope Paul VI**

The modern cult of physical health and beauty, with its vast commercial possibilities, seems to have been exploited to the very last limit of vulgarity. Has it helped us to appreciate the grace and dignity that proclaim the true quality of the queen?

The fact is, on the contrary, that minds and imaginations and emotions, nourished almost from infancy on this unsubstantial fare, must take a long, long step before they can understand why "all the beauty of the king's daughter is within," why the sweet and gentle Maid of Nazareth is "terrible as an army set in battle array," why she is the terror of the legions of hell whose proud leader she crushed beneath her foot, why she holds the destiny of nations in her hand, why, in a word, she is the Queen of the Universe. **Leo A. Pursley, D.D.**

She must always be before your eyes, my very dear daughters, that you may form your life on hers and make all your actions and affections correspond to hers. You are her daughters. Thus you must follow and imitate her, and make use of her example as of a mirror in which you look at yourself without ceasing. Even though the fragrance which you will receive by looking at and considering the life of Our Lady will fall into a vessel of clay, it will not lack an admirable sweetness, for balm put in earthen vessels is as sweet as that in a crystal vial. **St. Francis de Sales**

> *Mary, Glory of Womanhood,*
> *I also desire to be the handmaid of the Lord.*
> *Pray that I may complete my life's work*
> *as well as you did, and especially that*
> *I may receive God's grace to love others and*

to serve with a kind and generous heart.
Through Christ our Lord. Amen.

The Model Wife

Lady, who with tender word
Did keep the house of Christ the Lord,
Who set forth the bread and wine
Before the Living Wheat and Vine,
Reverently did make the bed
Whereon was laid the holy Head
That such a cruel pillow prest
For our behoof on Calvary's crest;
Be beside me while I go
About my labors to and fro.
Speed the wheel and speed the loom,
Guide the needle and the broom,
Make my bread rise sweet and light,
Make my cheese come foamy white;
Yellow may my butter be
As cowslips blowing on the lea.
Homely though my tasks and small,
Be beside me at them all.
Then when I stand face to face
Jesu in the judgment place,
To me thy gracious help afford,
Who art the Handmaid of the Lord.

"The Housewife's Prayer"
by Blanche Mary Kelly

With many women pursuing careers these days, the hidden life of a wife may seem less appealing. But God's design for marriage holds priceless treasures of unity in mind and heart, companionship and emotional support, and a common vision for home life and the raising of children. These are the foundation stones of a healthy and successful marriage. We can look to Mary and Joseph as a model couple in pursuing such marital intimacy and unity on a spiritual, emotional, and psychological level. In particular, they must have shared a common vision in the raising of Jesus.

As a wife and homemaker, Mary also shows us how the humdrum tasks of daily married life can be transformed by God's grace. Mary played a central role in making the home of the Holy Family a refuge of love, peace, and joy for her husband and Son. Her prayerful and attentive attitude of heart made her home a special place to all in Nazareth, especially their close circle of friends. By the grace of God, today's wife—whether a full-time career woman or homemaker—can imitate Mary as a role model without equal.

We know that Mary is a mother, but perhaps we have understood less well how truly she is a wife. This side of her life is not a game of make-believe, a convention, but an engagement fully lived out.... Mary loved Joseph as no other wife has loved her husband and Joseph was for her unclouded happiness. Their mutual love, lived in full harmony with their vocation, obtained its maximum strength, for the renouncing of all procreation, far from being in their case an obstacle to love, elevated and intensified it, as the banks of a river raise the waters which they canalize and control.   **Cardinal Léon Joseph Suenens**

"I was the Mother of God, but that did not excuse Me from being a respectful wife towards Joseph. He was a good, loving companion for Me and a watchful brother.... We loved one another, and we were concerned, in a holy way, with one thing only: our Son."   *Maria Valtorta's untranslated Notebooks of 1943*

Despite her glory in the eyes of God, to the people of Nazareth she was the carpenter's wife. Rather than making fanciful pictures of the life of Mary, it is perhaps best to stand amazed at this picture of emptying, of poverty.... The Second Vatican Council teaches that Mary "stands out among the poor and humble of the Lord who confidently hope for and receive salvation from him" (*Church*, 55). Her riches were totally in God.   **Christopher O'Donnell, O. Carm.**

A good wife who can find? She is far more precious than jewels. The heart of her husband trusts in her, and he will have no lack of gain. She does him good, and not harm, all the days of her life.... Strength and dignity are her clothing, and she laughs at the time to come. She opens her mouth with wisdom, and the teaching of kindness is on her tongue. She looks well to the ways of her household, and does not eat the bread of idleness.

Her children rise up and call her blessed; her husband also, and he praises her: "Many women have done excellently, but you surpass them all." Charm is deceitful, and beauty is vain, but a woman who fears the LORD is to be praised. Give her of the fruit of her hands, and let her works praise her in the gates.

Proverbs 31:10-12, 25-31

Mary's daily work was that of poor women in all times. It is this commonality that helps us see Mary as a model as wife, mother, cousin, daughter, or as the Model Relative in general. In our age of fragmented families, relationships are vulnerable to instantaneous severing. More than ever before mankind needs to find models of ongoing, successful relating. There is Mary. She moved among God's people recognizing and responding to the needs of others, all the others sent into her life by God's plan.

We find Mary in the ordinary, but the quality of peace present in her life was extraordinary. As wife, mother, daughter, friend, she was without sin. We work out our salvation in some or all of these relationships. Mary did it all, and she did it perfectly. Throughout her life, in joy and in sorrow, she kept her heart open to the Word of God. She remained obedient to his plan, full of grace.   **John Randall, S.T.D.**

As husband and wife, standing over the cradle of their newborn life forget, for the moment, the need of one another, so Mary and Joseph, in their possession of God in their family, hardly knew that they had bodies. Love usually makes husband and wife one; in the case of Mary and Joseph, it was not their combined loves but Jesus Who made them one. No deeper love ever beat under the roof of the world since the beginning, nor will it ever beat, even unto the end. They did not go to God through love of one another; rather, because they went first to God, they had a deep and pure love one for another.   **Fulton J. Sheen**

> *Mary, Glory of Womanhood,*
> *I also desire to be the handmaid of the Lord.*
> *Pray that I may complete my life's work*
> *as well as you did, and especially that*
> *I may receive God's grace to love others and*
> *to serve with a kind and generous heart.*
> *Through Christ our Lord. Amen.*

The Pattern of Motherhood

Mother! whose virgin bosom was uncrost
With the least shade of thought to sin allied;
Woman! above all women glorified,
Our tainted nature's solitary boast;
Purer than foam on central ocean tost;
Brighter than eastern skies at daybreak strewn
With fancied roses, than the unblemished moon
Before her wane begins on heaven's blue coast;
Thy Image falls to earth. Yet some, I ween
Not unforgiven the suppliant knee might bend,

As to a visible Power, in which did blend
All that was mixed and reconciled in Thee
Of mother's love with maiden purity,
Of high with low, celestial with terrene!

**"Sonnet to the Virgin"
by William Wordsworth**

Where would any of us be without a mother? A new life in the womb needs special care and protection to ever see the light of day. Newborn babies are absolutely dependent on someone to meet their needs, yet today many receive abuse instead of love. Let us look at Mary as an example of true motherly love, especially in the way in which she entrusted her only child to the care of God the Father.

This divine Mother is infinitely inferior to God, but immensely superior to all creatures; and as it is impossible to find a Son more noble than Jesus, so is it also impossible to find a Mother more noble than Mary. **St. Alphonsus**

The Curé of Ars used to say that the love of all mothers put together was but as ice in comparison of the mother's love of Mary, and this is not a hyperbole, or a mere rhetorical exaggeration, but an exact statement of what there is incomparable and universal in Mary's maternity, which remains the inexhaustible source of all maternal love here in this world.

Cardinal Léon Joseph Suenens

A human mother is an image of our Heavenly Mother, and she in turn is the image of God's own goodness, God's own heart.   **St. Maximilian Kolbe**

In Mary, God has chosen his own mother. How fitting that she be filled with grace from the first instant of her conception! From all eternity the Father predestined her to be the Theotokos, the mother of his own Son.   **Frederick M. Jelly, O.P.**

Under the tutelage of the Holy Spirit, Mary became strong with His strength, but this strength, at the same time, was clothed with the mantle of gentleness.

As Mary mothered the Church in its infancy, gentleness characterized her simple, strong, silent presence in her little family. Her gentleness brought hope and courage to this first Christian community. As the Mother of the Church, how gentle she was with the disciples who deserted her Son in His "hour" and how gentle her attitude to the repentant Peter who had denied his Master!

Only a strong woman could have "stood" beneath that cross on Calvary, but even this strength reflected a gentleness toward His executioners. She united herself totally with her Son as He prayed: "Father, forgive them; they do not know what they are doing" (Luke 23:34).   **David E. Rosage**

Mary did not measure God's love by His conformity to *her* plans nor even by the degree of financial or cultural success of her son. Unlike Mary, as a mother I find it easy to forget that my children are God's choice gifts to me and that He cares far more about them than I ever can! My greatest experience of love for them is but a dim shadow of His love for them.

June Miller

The love of God and the love of man, this is the twofold love that should inform the mind and will of all motherhood. It was this which was the secret of our Lady's serenity....

Other mothers, seeing such singular gifts as Christ must have had, such gifts of mind and body, such skill and such brilliance of thought, would surely have fretted if such a son had not shown more ambition, had not made a name for himself, why [should he] be a humble carpenter? For example, with his ability, and his imagination, he could become famous as a wood sculptor. Another mother would have complained that so brilliant a boy could surely better himself and her family fortune at the same time! Had she not seen with her own eyes that even the proud Rabbis were awed and silenced by his uncanny wisdom? Was it not the duty of such a son to provide a little comfort for his mother's old age?

But for Mary of Nazareth, it was enough that her son was about his Father's work. That is what he had said and his word was good enough for her. She knew that if he chose to be a poor working boy, absorbed in his trade, putting all that was in him into his humble job as an ordinary woodworker, if he was content and proud to bring home his labourer's pay towards their daily bread, then most certainly that was God's work. "He has put down the mighty from their seats and has exalted the humble."

Caryll Houselander

Mary was not ashamed by the fact that Jesus was scourged, that his face was spit upon, that he was treated as a leper, as one unwanted, despised, hated by all. Because he was Jesus, her son. And there surfaced the deep tenderness of her heart as a mother.

Mother Teresa of Calcutta

Motherhood means caring for the life of the child. Since Mary is the mother of us all, her care for the life of man is universal. The care of a mother embraces her child totally. Mary's motherhood has its beginning in her motherly care for Christ. In Christ, at the foot of the cross, she accepted John, and in John she accepted all of us totally.   **Joseph A. Pelletier, A.A.**

What does motherhood carry with it? Essentially, love and total willingness to serve. Those two things Catholics have always seen in Mary, telling her their needs with complete confidence, inwardly conversing with her freely.   **F. J. Sheed**

Mary is a *virgin* woman and mother. As such, her love for her children is never demanding or possessive. Never does she claim their love for herself. The sole object of her virgin maternal love is to lead her children to the love of Christ. All her motherly care is directed towards Christ.   **Edward Schillebeeckx, O.P.**

But she also had to suffer for our sakes as well as His. As Our Lord learned obedience by which He suffered, so Mary had to learn motherhood, not by appointment, but by experience with the burdens of the human heart. The rich cannot console the poor unless they become less rich for the sake of the poor; Mary cannot wipe away human tears unless she herself has been their fountain. The title "Mother of the Afflicted" had to be earned in the school of affliction.

Fulton J. Sheen

> *Mary, Glory of Womanhood,*
> *I also desire to be the handmaid of the Lord.*
> *Pray that I may complete my life's work*
> *as well as you did, and especially that*
> *I may receive God's grace to love others and*
> *to serve with a kind and generous heart.*
> *Through Christ our Lord. Amen.*

One Who Loves and Serves

And, if our faith had given us nothing more
Than this Example of all Womanhood,
So mild, so merciful, so strong, so good,
So patient, peaceful, loyal, loving, pure—
This were enough to prove it higher and truer

Than all the creeds the world had known before.
Virgin, who lovest the poor and lonely,
If the loud cry of a mother's heart
Can ever ascend to where thou art,
Into thy blessed hands and holy
Receive my prayer of praise and thanksgiving
Let the hands that bore our Savior bear it
Into the awful presence of God;
For thy feet with holiness are shod,
And, if thou bearest it, he will hear it.

"The Golden Legend"
by Henry Wadsworth Longfellow

Mary's response to the high praise of an angel and the overshadowing of the Holy Spirit was totally lacking in pride and pretense. Rather, she made haste to serve her cousin Elizabeth and to share the good news of the great love of God. Women are often given opportunities to love and serve others, whether in simple or profound ways. Let us recognize these occasions as wonderful gifts from God, and allow his love to flow forth through our actions.

In those days Mary arose and went with haste into the hill country, to a city of Judah, and she entered the house of Zechariah and greeted Elizabeth.... And Mary remained with her about three months, and returned to her home.   **Luke 1:39-40; 56**

Although Mary was chosen above all creatures to be the mother of God and the queen of heaven and earth, she nevertheless chose to be the handmaid of

God and of all the world. Therefore, when she had conceived our Lord, she went with great haste into the hill country to serve St. Elizabeth, the mother of St. John the Baptist, as her humble handmaid until the time when St. John was born.

Blessed John Ruusbroec

But Mary did not rest on her newly acquired dignity. The Lord's message had indicated to her a need: "Your cousin Elizabeth has in her old age, herself conceived a son." One who is in truth "servant of the Lord" is the servant of all who are the Lord's. With the fearlessness born of faith—even while knowing all the fears of the first hours of a first pregnancy—and impelled by love, the little girl from Nazareth sets out across the alien land of the Samaritans into the sophistication of suburbia to offer her humble service.

M. Basil Pennington, O.C.S.O.

At first glance, Mary seems to have had a choice: to stay at Nazareth and "love the Lord her God," newly conceived in her womb, or to "love her neighbor" by visiting Elizabeth. Really, there was no choice. One can choose only between two separable things. The love of God and of neighbor are as inseparable as the sun and the light of day: the one brings on and sustains and requires the other. All love is a seamless robe. If anyone says "I love God," and loves not his brother, he is a liar. Mary went to Elizabeth because she loved her neighbor and, because she loved God so much, she went in a hurry.

Fr. Payton's Rosary Prayer Book

Mary said: "Let it be done according to thy word." Then she went in haste. See her total surrender. This is why Our Lady is a Missionary of Charity in the true sense of the word. Our Lady spent nine months with Jesus; Jesus was in her... and what did she do? Scrub, clean, [and] wash, but she really loved her total surrender. **Mother Teresa of Calcutta**

Love is patient and kind; love is not jealous or boastful; it is not arrogant or rude. Love does not insist on its own way; it is not irritable or resentful; it does not rejoice at wrong, but rejoices in the right. Love bears all things, believes all things, hopes all things, endures all things. **1 Corinthians 13:4-7**

All we know about Our Lady's life after the Crucifixion, is that the disciple John took her to live with him. "From that hour that disciple took her into his own home." There, in secrecy again, she lived what is certainly our life of preparation for heaven; in secrecy, but known to all those around her, as every Christian is.

In the first Advent, she had prepared to look upon the face of her Son by working for Joseph: cooking, cleaning, weaving, mending for him, and undoubtedly being a companion to him in thought, too. Now she had come to another Advent, a preparation for seeing her Son's face in heaven, and it was to be lived out in exactly the same way.   **Caryll Houselander**

The Mother of Jesus is a perfect model of prayer because she knew from her own personal experience what the power of the Holy Spirit could work in the lives of these first followers of her divine Son. She showed her loving concern for the members of the first Christian family who were to be the messengers of the "good news of great joy" to a waiting world. Her complete union with God as the special temple of the Holy Spirit caused her to radiate God's loving and abiding presence to those near her....

Her life was a life of love translated into giving to others. She gave herself unstintingly to her family at Nazareth, on Calvary, and to the infant Christian community. By her thoughts and words, by her attitudes and actions, Mary personified the Spirit of love radiating through her. In this she taught us how we too must respond in giving ourselves lovingly and graciously.   **David E. Rosage**

Scripture gives us nothing of the Spirit-giving occasions that occurred in Mary's life at Nazareth in her relationships with her relatives, friends, and fellow villagers. But her solicitude at the wedding feast of Cana would lead us to imagine that she went about doing good, impelled by that inner power of the Holy Spirit's love. For one as sensitive to the presence of the Spirit, Mary must have been a quiet, loving force in Nazareth. Her radiant beauty and humility must have attracted her fellow villagers to her humble home. Her days must have been filled with gentle ways of doing good in little ways, often unnoticed by others, except the one who felt the presence of the Holy Spirit of God passing from Mary to him or to her as Mary performed some act of kindness.

George Maloney, S.J.

We also discover the genuine Mary, full of tenderness, in the wedding feast at Cana. She was moved by seeing the newlyweds exposed to the humiliation of not having wine. That is why she said to Jesus, "They have no more wine."

I think this is the wonderful tenderness of a woman's heart: to be aware of the suffering of others and to try to spare them that suffering, as Mary did. Do you and I have that same tenderness in our hearts? Do we have Mary's eyes for discovering the needs of others? **Mother Teresa of Calcutta**

Mary is not only the great instance of the contemplative life, but also of the practical. Mary was as full of external work and hard service as any religious Sister in this day. Of course her duties varied according to the seasons of her life, as a young maiden, as a wife, as a mother, and as a widow; but still her life was full of duties day by day and hour by hour.

Cardinal John Henry Newman

To love God above all things is the first commandment; to love the neighbor above all that is not God is the reflection of the first commandment (Matthew 22:37-39). The most holy Virgin, our glorious Mistress, practiced both these loves in the reception she gave to her Son. She loved Him and received Him as her God, and she received Him, loved Him, and served Him as her neighbor. We cannot have one of the loves without the other (1 John 4:20-21).

St. Francis de Sales

> *Mary, Glory of Womanhood,*
> *I also desire to be the handmaid of the Lord.*
> *Pray that I may complete my life's work*
> *as well as you did, and especially that*
> *I may receive God's grace to love others and*
> *to serve with a kind and generous heart.*
> *Through Christ our Lord. Amen.*

Full of Grace and Wisdom

Spilled all about her, pooled in radiance,
The guardian brightness of God's favor lay,
Like light, too luminous to bear the trace
Of shadow, too intense, too strong for sight.
No vision here is ours. Nor Gabriel's,

Who, shaded in his sanctity, was sent
To stand here, lonely and apart, to speak
In whisper that which only God could see.
Hail, full of grace, the Lord is with thee:
Blessed art thou among women.   **John Lynch**

The secret of Mary's life was grace, pure grace. And her response to God's grace was one of absolute abandon. Mary's complete openness to the Holy Spirit allowed her to receive God's wisdom without the distortion of sin. Mary fully received God's grace and wisdom through the Holy Spirit, and then served as a vessel for that grace and wisdom to touch those around her.

Of all women, of all purely human beings, she was and is the most alive. She is all in God and God is all in her and so does she confront forever the nothingness of death, of sin.

Mary is all in God and God is all in her by grace. In this consists her splendor, her perfection. Grace is the reality in Mary by which her soul was pleasing to God; indeed, of all created spirits the most pleasing. By the grace of the virtues her every capacity was turned to God, dedicated to and absorbed by His love and service. By the grace of the gifts of the Holy Ghost Mary was ready, even eager, to live by every illumination, every inspiration of the Spirit who was to be her Spouse.   **Ferrer Smith, O.P.**

Blessed be Mary for her faith in God's grace; she had but one concern in life, the grace of her Christ. Except through grace alone, nothing was to affect her. And the trials and tribulations still remaining to her were but channels of grace, and again, grace; splashes from the tide that washed over her life's beginning, and was to flow in ever increasing volume up to that final hour, with the Assumption of the Blessed Virgin Mary into heaven.   **Josef Weiger**

Hail, full of grace! In her womb was the grace of divinity, in her heart the grace of charity, upon her lips the grace of courtesy, in her hands the grace of mercy and generosity. And she was truly full of grace, for her captives have received redemption, the sick their cure, the sorrowful their comfort, and sinners their pardon; the just have received grace, the angels joy, and the Blessed Trinity glory and honor, and the Son of Man the substance of human flesh.   **St. Bernard**

As His Son was to be the perfect Man, so the Woman would have to be filled with grace—never offending Him, always seeking Him, ever an obedient daughter. What a marvel He must create—a finite creature—a weak woman—but so pure and immaculate that His own Son would find a suitable dwelling in which to become Man.   **Mother Angelica**

Certainly she would have been a frail being, like Eve, without the grace of God. A more abundant gift of grace made her what she was from the first. There was no difference in kind between her and us, though an inconceivable difference of degree. She and we are both simply saved by the grace of Christ.... Can we refuse to see that Mary was a *typical woman* like Eve, that both were endowed with special gifts of grace, and that Mary succeeded where Eve failed?

Cardinal John Henry Newman

Our Lord Jesus brought our Lady Saint Mary to my understanding. I saw her spirituality in her bodily likeness, a simple, humble maiden, young in years, grown a little taller than a child, of the stature which she had when she conceived. Also God showed me part of the wisdom and the truth of her soul, and in this I understood the reverent contemplation with which she beheld her God....

And this wisdom and truth, this knowledge of her Creator's greatness and of her own created littleness, made her say very meekly to Gabriel: Behold me here, God's handmaiden. In this sight I understood truly that she is greater, more worthy and more fulfilled than everything else which God has created, and which is inferior to her. Above her is no created thing, except the blessed humanity of Christ.

Vision of Julian of Norwich

Now, always to be awake, guarded, fervent, so as to be able to act not only without sin, but in the best possible way, in the varying circumstances of each day, denotes a life of untiring mindfulness. But of such a life, Prudence [Wisdom] is the presiding virtue.   **Cardinal John Henry Newman**

Mary is called the Seat of Wisdom because she was attuned to God. The Holy Spirit was poured into her so fully that the Son of God took flesh in her womb. She became pregnant with God and gave him to the world, conceiving him, as Augustine said, in her mind before her flesh.   **John Randall, S.T.D.**

Mary, Glory of Womanhood,
I also desire to be the handmaid of the Lord.
Pray that I may complete my life's work
as well as you did, and especially that
I may receive God's grace to love others and
to serve with a kind and generous heart.
Through Christ our Lord. Amen.

FOUR

A Mother's Prayers

Perhaps Mary is most widely recognized in her role of intercessor, an obvious expression of her motherly concern for her children's welfare. Countless Christians over the centuries have sought refuge in Mary when faced with difficulties or dangers. In times of war or crisis, when whole nations turn to God in prayer, many rosaries are prayed to Mary.

Whenever I think about the pain, sorrow, and suffering in the world, I am filled with grief. Yet Jesus and Mary see it all. They both lived among us. They know our griefs. They understand. Then why don't their hearts of love break? Because they see with the eyes of faith and hope.

Jesus died to set us free from the bondage of sin. In her intercession to Jesus, Mary pours her efforts into strengthening us with the grace of God which alone brings healing, restoration, and salvation. Mary knows that our eternal destinies are at stake, and that

Satan will be defeated in the end. She knows that a glorious reunion awaits the sons and daughters of God.

The wedding at Cana initiated our mother's bold intercession on our behalf. Mary's sensitivity to the needs of the hosts illustrates her attentiveness to the smallest details of our lives. Her readiness to turn to Jesus and ask his help bears witness to her intercessor's heart. In utter simplicity, she turns the difficulty over to her Son. Mary loves each of us in the same way today. United to Christ and through his saving power, she brings our needs to the Father.

Mary Brings Our Needs to the Father

She dries her children's tears as mothers do,
And pours a draught of grace from prayer-cupped
    hands,
That each may journey back refreshed and glad
To better lands.

O Virgin, let thy fleet compassion's spark
Light up the murky paths we stumble on;
Give us the warmth of thy embrace when earth's
Cold pain is gone.   **"Hymn for Second Vespers: Feast of
the Apparition of Our Lady of Lourdes"
(from the Latin by Raymond F. Roseliep)**

On the third day there was a marriage at Cana in Galilee, and the mother of Jesus was there; Jesus also was invited to the marriage, with his disciples. When the wine gave out, the mother of Jesus said to him, "They have no wine." And Jesus said to her, "O woman, what have you to do with me? My hour has not yet come." His mother said to the servants, "Do whatever he tells you."   **John 2:1-5**

Mary is the loving heart in our lives. She is objective and even matter-of-fact, but, because she has herself experienced and shared them, she always understands our difficulties in life and has sympathy for us. With unfailing solicitude she finds out what our needs are and, with the straightforward simplicity of a mother, she brings them to the attention of God who, in Jesus, was and still is her Child, her "Boy" — "They have no wine!"

If only we could spend but one single moment listening to Mary's wordless conversation about us with Jesus! If we could but catch a single glimpse of her face when she looks at her Son with a glance which tells him, "They have no wine," "They have no money," "They are in terrible distress," "Their father is ill and their mother has eight children already...."   **Edward Schillebeeckx, O.P.**

In Cana Mary made her first public intercession. In a sisterly way she saw to it that the bridal pair and their guests were happy and contented, and kept an eye on the domestic arrangements. She was thus the first to notice that the wine was running out. Unobtrusively she turned to her Son. **Josef Weiger**

This is another of my favorite scenes. One might ask whatever possessed Mary to go to Christ with this particular need. I can feel for our Lord and well understand His seemingly enigmatic answer that has kept the Scripture scholars busy. Things were not transpiring exactly as He might have planned. "After all, Mother, do you want it to go down in history that the first sign the Son of God worked on his saving mission was to turn out more booze for the boys after they had drunk the house dry?"

M. Basil Pennington, O.C.S.O.

At the Marriage Feast of Cana, Mary had an opportunity to keep the love of her Son to herself alone. She had the choice of continuing to be only the Mother of Jesus. But she knew that she must not keep that love for herself alone under the penalty of never enjoying love to the fullest. If she would save Jesus, she must lose Him. So she asked Him to work His first miracle, to begin His public life, and to anticipate the HOUR—and that means His Passion and Death. **Fulton J. Sheen**

The marriage feast at Cana repeats itself constantly in heaven. Mary has only to suggest to Jesus that he intervene to be lavishly answered. When we turn to her in prayer, she turns to her Son and says: "My child has need of you." She does not have to tell him what we need. She simply turns us over to Jesus, as she turned the problem of the dwindling wine over to him at the wedding feast. She knows he will give her children the wine they need, choice wine in superabundance.

Cana repeats itself in heaven to the fullest degree. Mary's ever vigilant love anticipates our pleas. She turns to Jesus for us even before we think of turning to her.   **Joseph A. Pelletier, A.A.**

Mary is the mother of all men and of all peoples, even *before* they come to faith in Christ. When Christian missionaries come to a hitherto unknown missionary territory they find that Mary has already been there for a long time, and that she has already filled the water-pots with water and is only waiting for the priests who will follow her and bring about the miracle of Cana in Christ's name.

Edward Schillebeeckx, O.P.

For taken up to Heaven, she did not lay aside this saving role, but by her manifold acts of intercession, continues to win for us gifts of eternal salvation. By her maternal charity, Mary cares for the brethren of her Son who still journey on earth, surrounded by dangers and difficulties.

Vatican II, "Lumen Gentium," No. 62

Who did ever return home bereft of joy, after having entreated Mary, Mother of God, on behalf of his needs? **St. Amadeus**

Such is Mary's greatness, so powerful is her favor with God, that not to have recourse to her in times of need is like trying to fly without wings. **Pope Leo XIII**

She is easily found by those who seek her. **Wisdom 6:12**

No one has access to the Almighty as His Mother has; none has merit such as hers. Her Son will deny her nothing that she asks; and herein lies her power. While she defends the Church, neither height nor depth, neither men nor evil spirits, neither great monarchs, nor craft of man, nor popular violence, can avail to harm us; for human life is short, but Mary reigns above, a Queen for ever.

Cardinal John Henry Newman

If then, O brethren, you desire consolation in every labor, have recourse to Mary; invoke the name of Mary, honor Mary, recommend yourselves to Mary, rejoice with Mary, weep with Mary, pray with Mary, walk with Mary, seek Jesus with Mary; in fine, desire to live and die with Jesus and Mary. By acting thus you will always advance in the ways of God, for Mary will most willingly pray for you, and the Son will most certainly grant all that his Mother asks.

Thomas à Kempis

Let us ask our dear Mother and Queen, then, to purify, sanctify, and beautify every little gift we present to her, and thus make it worthy of God.

All that our soul possesses is of less value—in the matter of winning God's friendship and favor—than a worm-eaten apple presented by a poor farmer to a king as rental for his farm.

But suppose this poor farmer knew the queen, and was well liked by her. And suppose he was a wise farmer. Would he not give his apple to the queen, that she might put it before the king?

The queen, out of kindness to the man who had only this to give, and out of respect for the king, would remove all the bad spots from the apple, place it in a gold dish, and surround it with flowers before she handed it to the king.

Would His Majesty refuse to accept the apple then? Would he not receive it with joy from the hands of His queen? **St. Louis de Montfort**

While nature itself made the name of mother the sweetest of all names, and has made motherhood the very model of tender and foresighted love, no tongue is eloquent to put in words what every devout soul feels, namely, how intense is the flame of affectionate and active charity which burns in Mary, in her who is truly our Mother not in a human way but through Christ....

Accordingly, let us approach Mary boldly, wholeheartedly beseeching her by the bonds of her motherhood which unite her so closely to Jesus and at the same time to us; let us with deepest devotion invoke her constant aid in the prayer which she herself has indicated and which is most acceptable to her; then with good reason shall we rest with an easy and joyous mind under the protection of this best of mothers.

Pope Leo XII

There are some naive minds that regard our Lady as more merciful than the Lord. Through childish judgment, they reach the conclusion that the Lord is more severe than she, and that we need to have recourse to our Lady because otherwise the Lord will punish us. It is true that our Lady is entrusted with the very special office of interceding for us, but the source of all goodness is the Lord. Christ is the one Mediator, the one font of grace. Our Lady herself is dependent upon Christ for all that she possesses. **Pope Paul VI**

On May 5, 1917, Pope Benedict XV wrote a memorable letter lamenting "the cruel war, the suicide of Europe." Only eight days before our Lady's appearance at Fatima, he included this appeal for Christians everywhere to pray to Mary for peace:

"To Mary, then, who is the Mother of Mercy and omnipotent by grace, let loving and devout appeal go up from every corner of the earth—from noble temples and tiniest chapels, from royal palaces and mansions of the rich as from the poorest hut—from every place wherein a faithful soul finds shelter—

from blood-drenched plains and seas. Let it bear to her the anguished cry of mothers and wives, the wailing of innocent little ones, the sighs of every generous heart: that her most tender and benign solicitude may be moved and the peace we ask for be obtained for our agitated world." **Pope Benedict XV**

> *Mary, compassionate mother*
> *and refuge of sinners,*
> *you know my trials and sorrows.*
> *Present my needs to the Father*
> *and come to my aid in the battle.*
> *Draw me ever nearer to Jesus your Son.*
> *Through Christ our Lord. Amen.*

Mary Draws Us Nearer to God

Slowly wending Her way
Through a world of twilight,
Darkness, poverty, and ruin,
Our Lady gathers Her seventh joy—
The souls that loved Her
In the darkness of the inhumanity
That men can show to men;
The souls that still remembered
To say, once in a while,
The Hail Mary,
Or just to invoke Her
By Her first name—Mary.
At eventide She will return—

The resplendent Mother of God
Dressed in an ordinary
Jewish woman's working clothes
That blend miraculously
With every age and clime
And even enter
Our present year of grace—
At eventide She will return
To Her heavenly domain.   **Catherine de Hueck Doherty**

Mary's only purpose is to draw us nearer to God the Father, to call us into the heart of God the Son, and to release in us the power of God the Holy Spirit. The deepest desire of this best of all mothers is to see all of her children finally in the courts of heaven, where she can fully embrace us and welcome us home.

Mary is not set between Christ and ourselves to keep us at a distance from him, but she is precisely the means chosen by God in order that there may be no distance between us, and that we may be sure of drawing near to him....

In proportion as our union with Mary increases, not only will she put into our hearts this or that disposition which she has taken from Jesus, but she will give us her own heart with which to love Him. This is her only thought and her only purpose. To give Jesus to every soul and to the whole world is still the only ambition of this incomparable mother.

Cardinal Léon Joseph Suenens

We speak to Mary to come to Jesus. She brought Him into the world; she is the mother of Jesus; she presents us to Him if we are devoted to her. **Pope Paul VI**

Mary is our most reliable guide to Christ, the person in the best position to attest to the truth of Christ, precisely because she is his mother. She knows him as no one else among us possibly can. And because God was able to entrust his only Son to her, her Son has been able to entrust us to her guidance. When Mary counsels every one of us to "Do whatever he tells you," she is assuring us that we can entrust ourselves to him. **Dr. Joyce A. Little**

When we invoke Mary, we bring her ever nearer to the hearth which sets her ablaze, we unite her more closely to her only love. For when we say: "The Lord is with thee, blessed art thou among women," she turns joyfully towards Him who is with her and pours out His blessings upon her. As our poor laboured *Aves* go up to her, Mary transforms them into hymns to God, triumphant doxologies.
Cardinal Léon Joseph Suenens

Mary is totally related to Jesus. She is entirely bound up with him. She has no meaning without him. Her mission, her role in God's plan is to draw us to Jesus so that we may give ourselves more completely to him in love and service. We must go to Mary in order to be led more effectively to Jesus. The Madonna, the mother with the Child in her arms, represents the true Mary, the Mary we should honor and pray.

Joseph A. Pelletier, A.A.

The Holy Spirit uses the holy mother as a primary instrument in awakening persons to the mysteries of the faith and in deepening their union with the Lord.... In the Gospels of Matthew, Luke, and John particularly we see Mary as a key instrument of the Holy Spirit not merely in the enfleshing of the Word physically, as it were, but also in being the first, and in some ways the best, human resonance of the divine initiative, the first ripple to the plunging of God into the waters of humanity, the good soil that first receives the seed, God's word, and feeds it with human love and life. In so doing, she becomes the Spirit's model for what he is about in every human soul and in the church at large. She is response and instrument. **George Montague, S.M.**

It is easier to understand the meek and humble heart of Christ by looking at His Mother. She holds all the great Truths of Christianity together, as a piece of wood holds a kite. Children wrap the string of a kite around a stick, and release the string as the kite climbs to the heavens.

Mary is that piece of wood. Around her we wrap all the precious strings of the great Truths of our holy Faith—for example, the Incarnation, the Eucharist, the Church. No matter how far we get above the earth, as the kite may, we always have need of Mary to hold the doctrines of the Creed together.

If we threw away the stick, we would no longer have the kite; if we threw away Mary, we would never have Our Lord. He would be lost in the Heavens, like our runaway kite, and that would be terrible, indeed, for us on earth. **Fulton J. Sheen**

If it is true, in a mystical sense, that Christ will hang from the cross while a single soul remains to be saved, so it is true that Mary will stand beneath the cross in the travail of her motherhood until all her children are counted in the courts of heaven.
Leo A. Pursley, D.D.

Through Mary's intercession, many souls are in paradise who would not be there had she not interceded for them, for God has entrusted her with the keys and treasures of the heavenly Kingdom.
St. Thomas Aquinas

Mary remains ever the path that leads to Christ.
Pope Paul VI

Mary, compassionate mother
and refuge of sinners,
you know my trials and sorrows.
Present my needs to the Father
and come to my aid in the battle.
Draw me ever nearer to Jesus your Son.
Through Christ our Lord. Amen.

Mary Is One of Us

Mother, who knew
what hardship shakes
a woman bundling clothes
and putting by her wheaten cakes:
Mother who urged the donkey
(making happy riot
on the straggling stones),
urged the beast to be more quiet;
Mother who heard the Child
whimper beneath the thin blue shawl,
our aching prayers cry out to thee.
Mother, pray for them all.

A thousand Bethlehems
mask dark tonight;
the eyes of little friendly homes
have lost their light;
pathetic heaps of poor dear things
are laid aside; a small bird sings
where a latched door swings.
Mother, whose sad Egyptian flight
preceded all of these,
guide them in faith beneath familiar stars—
Our Lady of the Refugees.   **"Our Lady of the Refugees"**
                               by Sister Mary Maura

*Mary is often glorified and put on a pedestal in our
minds and hearts, so pure that she is considered out of*

reach to us common mortals. As these readings will show, Mary is very human, very much a woman of flesh, approachable in every way. We do her a great injustice to hold our mother at arm's length—afraid that she will not be able to bear the stench of our sins.

The Blessed Virgin Mary has, before us, trodden the straight and narrow path which leads to sanctity; before us she has carried the cross, before us she has known the ascents of the spirit through suffering. Sometimes, perhaps, we do not dare to look at Jesus the God-Man, who because of His divinity seems too far above us; but near Him is Mary, His Mother and our Mother, a privileged creature surely, yet a creature like ourselves, and therefore a model more accessible for our weakness.

Gabriel of St. Mary Magdalen, O.C.D.

At last, a human being on this earth, an authentic, real human being, not an imaginary character in a novel, not the mere postulate of an ideal system of ethics, but a person of flesh and blood, with tears, toil, poverty, obscurity, but who is, wholly and utterly, purity, kindness, love, faithfulness, patience, compassion, and belongs to God alone.... Yet all this splendor was confined and hidden in the sober, unassuming, ordinary ways of a human being such as we know only too well, and suffer from.

Karl Rahner

What loving-kindness of God! With this greeting He gave Mary the confirmation: the angelic salutation really was a message from Him. And so He strengthened Mary in all the fears and doubts that assailed her soul at the prospect of the shame and disgrace that awaited her. When Elizabeth said, "Blessed is the fruit of your womb!" a feeling of relief would have swept over Mary. This was no natural fruit that she bore but a blessed fruit—the very Son of God. For Mary it must have been like a new and gracious salutation from God Himself, confirming her calling and dispelling all her perplexity and inner conflict.

Basilea Schlink

Mary's "angelic purity"—that poetic phrase is a misfortune. It makes Mary a little unapproachable. Purity is not an angelic virtue—it cannot be, since angels have no bodies. It is a human virtue, and Mary's purity was very human. So human, in fact, that, like all else human, it would not have been perfect without grace. *Fr. Payton's Rosary Prayer Book*

The immaculate conception does not make Mary distant from us; on the contrary, she comes closer. Sin dehumanizes. Mary, the sinless one, is more fully human. Similarly, the more sinless we are, the more compassionate we can be. This may seem paradoxical, but it can be daily verified in practice: the more we sin, the less kind we tend to be toward others who fail.

Mary, being without sin, can truly be a compassionate mother in our sinfulness.

Christopher O'Donnell, O. Carm.

Why should human frailty fear to go to Mary? In her there is no austerity, nothing terrible: she is all sweetness, offering milk and wool to all. **St. Bernard**

Our Lady is seen as fully human. She is not equated with divinity, because she is essentially representative of humanity. She is not on a par with God the Redeemer, because she personifies man the redeemed. In her we glimpse not so much God's design for a single human being, as His plan for all human beings. **Walter J. Burghardt, S.J.**

God is everywhere; but nowhere is He closer to us, and more adapted to our humanity, than in Mary. It was to make Himself nearer and dearer to us that He came to dwell in her. Everywhere else He is the Bread of the strong, the Bread of the angels. In Mary He is the Bread of the little ones. **St. Louis de Montfort**

Mary, in fact, is one of our race, a true daughter of Eve—though free of that mother's sin—and truly our sister, who as a poor and humble woman fully shared our lot. **Pope Paul VI**

This perfect model is also *wonderfully attractive*. First, Mary is a mere creature as we are, a sister, a mother whom we are drawn to imitate that we may show her our gratitude, our veneration, and our love. Then, she is a model *easy* of imitation in this way that she sanctified herself in the ordinary, everyday life common to most of us, by fulfilling those lowly household duties of a young woman and a mother, leading a hidden, retired life both in joy and in sorrow, in the heights of exaltation and in the deepest humiliations. We are on firm ground when we imitate the Blessed Virgin. It is the best way of imitating Jesus and of obtaining Mary's all-powerful intercession.

Adolphe Tanquerey

To save men from their sins is a great mercy of God; but to save this one woman from ever sinning was a greater mercy, but still a mercy. Not only that. Sinless as she was, possessed of grace at every instant, she was still a member of a fallen race, a race to which heaven was closed. The Savior's redeeming act opened heaven to her as to all members of the race.

F. J. Sheed

Mary, compassionate mother
and refuge of sinners,
you know my trials and sorrows.
Present my needs to the Father
and come to my aid in the battle.
Draw me ever nearer to Jesus your Son.
Through Christ our Lord. Amen.

Finding Jesus in the Temple

"My exaltation to afflictions high!
Afflicted I may be, it seems, and blest!
I will not argue that nor will repine.
But where delays he now? Some great intent
Conceals him. When twelve years he scarce had
    seen,
I lost him, but so found as well I saw
He could not lose himself, but went about
His Father's business. What he meant I mused—
Since understand; much more his absence now
Thus long to some great purpose he obscures.
But I to wait with patience am inured;
My heart hath been a storehouse long of things
And sayings laid up, portending strange events."
    Thus Mary, pondering oft, and oft to mind
Recalling what remarkably had passed
Since first her salutation heard, with thoughts
Meekly composed awaited the fulfilling.
                    Paradise Regained by John Milton

*Mary appeared so unexceptional and ordinary to those
around her that she is only mentioned along with the other
women and Jesus' relations in Acts 1:14. One very concrete
example of Mary's humanity is the story of losing Jesus
and then finding him in the temple. Let us consider Mary's
fears and struggles as she and Joseph tried to find their only
Son who had been lost in Jerusalem for three days.*

Now his parents went to Jerusalem every year at the feast of the Passover. And when he was twelve years old, they went up according to custom; and when the feast was ended, as they were returning, the boy Jesus stayed behind in Jerusalem.

His parents did not know it, but supposing him to be in the company they went a day's journey, and they sought him among their kinsfolk and acquaintances; and when they did not find him, they returned to Jerusalem, seeking him. After three days they found him in the temple, sitting among the teachers, listening to them and asking them questions; and all who heard him were amazed at his understanding and his answers.

And when they saw him they were astonished; and his mother said to him, "Son, why have you treated us so? Behold, your father and I have been looking for you anxiously." And he said to them, "How is it that you sought me? Did you not know that I must be in my Father's house?" And they did not understand the saying which he spoke to them. And he went down with them and came to Nazareth, and was obedient to them; and his mother kept all these things in her heart. **Luke 2:41-51**

The holy life of the blessed Virgin is startlingly like our own. She lived what, viewed from the outside, was a really commonplace and obscure life, enduring the ordinary petty round of any average woman in any odd corner of a small country, far from the great stream of history, of civilization, and of politics. She set off on a search, she felt anxious, she did not know everything either. She wept, she had to ask her way and seek her way from stage to stage of her life's journey, like other human beings.   **Karl Rahner**

The first remark on the anxious mother's lips after those frustrating days of search was one that any human mother would have uttered out of sheer relief. At that moment, Mary shared our frailty. And indeed, humanly speaking, a life that never let a plaintive sigh rise to heaven would be beyond belief.

The life of every saint proceeds from light into darkness and darkness into light. Mary's is no exception. But when she found her Child, was her behavior perfect? Perfection is not incompatible with frailty. Mary was perfect when the annunciation angel bowed down before her, and so she was in the Temple when her heart unburdened itself in an impetuous question. Perfection is not conspicuous for its lack of spontaneity, its taciturnity, or a self-conscious restraint of emotions which may be sincere and genuine. God is concerned with hearts.

Josef Weiger

Christ suffered the sense of the loss of God, of being left, *forsaken* by God. Our Lady, therefore, suffered the same thing: the sense of the loss of God. And of all the sufferings of human nature, this is the most universal and the most purifying.

Therefore she lived through this strange, baffling thing for the love of God and for the love of us; she suffered it in Christ because Christ suffers it in human nature.

We have seen that her "Be it done unto me according to thy word" is uttered again in His "Not my will, but thine be done." Just so is her "Son, why hast thou done so to us?" repeated in His "My God, My God, why has thou forsaken me?"

Everyone experiences this sense of the loss of the Divine Child.   **Caryll Houselander**

As the wonder of God's life in us and the working of His power through us become a settled fact in our lives, we can, in spite of the wonder, begin to take it for granted. "God is with me. Things should be as they are. After all God is God, and he loves me. So it is."

I have been strongly struck by the words of the Gospel: "They *assumed* he was with them." All the more shock then when suddenly the awful truth strikes home: He is not with us. Then the pain, the agony, the fear, the self-questioning. The fumbling through the dark may last more than three days and nights. But if we persevere in the seeking we will at last come to at least that much of a perception of His presence that we can cry out: "Why have you done this...?"

This seemingly strange pericope of Jesus' twelve-year-old escapade has something very important to teach us. And as we struggle with the experience it illumines, it is good to know that Mary has been through it, too, in her own way and so can understand and show us the way.

M. Basil Pennington, O.C.S.O.

Later on, she was again seeking for Christ, this time among the crowd that thronged round Him in His public life. She is among those who are trying to get close to Him: therefore, she is among the sick, the crippled, the blind, the poorest beggars—outcasts of every description. For such are the people who follow Christ in every age.

It is just like Our Lady, this: she, who did not seek an exalted or solitary life in which to prepare for Christ's birth, is content now to follow Him in the crowd, to seek Him among strangers in the public street. **Caryll Houselander**

> *Mary, compassionate mother*
> *and refuge of sinners,*
> *you know my trials and sorrows.*
> *Present my needs to the Father*
> *and come to my aid in the battle.*
> *Draw me ever nearer to Jesus your Son.*
> *Through Christ our Lord. Amen.*

Refuge of Sinners

Repentant sinners do not know the glory
That covers the Woman who waits for them.
They run, stumble, fall at Her feet.
They see only a mother,
And washing Her feet with their tears,
They call out—"Oh, Mother!"

Gently, She lifts up the tangled hair.
Lo and behold! It shines.
The uplifted face of the repentant sinner,
Cupped in Her hands,
Becomes one that the angels
Must veil their faces
To look at.   **Catherine de Hueck Doherty**

"Refuge of sinners, pray for us." This is one of the most beautiful invocations in the Litany of Loreto. In the second half of the Hail Mary, we pray: "Pray for us sinners, now and at the hour of our death." Sinners need a refuge, one who will constantly intercede on our behalf. Let us run and fall at Mary's feet, crying out, "Oh, Mother!"

What shall I do when tempted by the flesh? Have the Virgin for your advocate, who is a fragrance of sweet smelling incense.... She has the fragrance of myrrh that destroys the worms of corruption. If you are devoted to her, you will feel temptations melting away, like wax before the fire.   **St. John of Avila**

Whoever is in the night of sin, let him cast his eyes on the moon, let him implore Mary.   **Pope Innocent III**

When the waves of pride or ambition sweep over you, when the tide of detraction or jealousy runs against you, look up to the Star, call upon Mary! When the shipwreck of avarice, anger, or lust seems imminent, call upon Mary!

If the horror of sin overwhelms you and the voice of conscience terrifies you, if the fear of judgment, the abyss of sadness, and the depths of despair clutch at your heart, think of Mary! In dangers, difficulties, and doubts, think about Mary, call upon Mary!   **St. Bernard**

Blessed assurance, safe refuge, the Mother of God is our mother. The mother of him in whom alone we have hope, whom alone we fear, is our mother. The mother of him who alone saves and condemns is our mother.   **St. Anselm**

I am the city of refuge, says Our Lady, for all those who have recourse to me. Come, then, to me, my children; for [through] me you will obtain graces, and in greater abundance than you can possibly imagine.
St. John Damascene

When a mother sees her sons going astray or behaving badly, she does not cease to love them. One might say that she loves them all the more, because in addition to her natural affection she develops a sense of anxious compassion for them when she thinks of the way in which they have risked their eternal salvation by sinning. Mary's attitude to us is like this.   **Cardinal Antonio Bacci**

Mary is not only the mother of those who have reached a high level of mystical experience in their lives. She is also, in a certain sense, the *special* mother of those who are still caught up in the habits of sin. It was by God's exceptional mercy that she remained unacquainted with sin, and without this mercy she would never have been immaculate. For this reason, she shows her gratitude to God by taking on the function of "Refuge of Sinners." ... The sinner who looks up to Mary for help can hope to be liberated from his sinful situation. She is our advocate, the one to whom we appeal for help in every difficult situation. She is our life, our sweetness, our hope.

Edward Schillebeeckx, O.P.

Are we anything but wretched lost sinners who, through cowardly self-pity, are not willing to recognize this, and prefer to blame God's providence rather than our sins? If then we look at Mary, refuge of sinners, we must indeed say that she was the only entirely sinless [human] person in the world. But her life, poor, insignificant, modest, sorrowful, gives us solace after all, and the strong hope that we are more than merely sinners, that God's grace is doing in us what it did in her. **Karl Rahner**

She entered fully into her Son's intentions, assumed the heart of a mother for all sinners, and looked upon them as the children of sorrow whom she had brought forth at the foot of the cross. Thus that sea of sufferings into which Jesus and Mary were plunged has become for sinners a river of peace and a fountain of blessings. **Venerable Thomas of Jesus**

And while Mary never experienced our weakness and the defect of our fallen nature, she, the best and most devoted of mothers, nonetheless knows them. With what opportuneness and generosity will she not come to our aid! With what tenderness she will console us! And with what strength she will sustain us! Travelling the road which the sacred Blood of Christ and Mary's tears have consecrated, we shall certainly and easily come to share in their most blessed glory. **Pope Leo XIII**

Amid the fiery splendor of all the glorious seraphim, Mary was crowned Queen of heaven's Angels and Saints. But she is the Immaculate Queen of earthly *sinners* as well. The world is full of her prodigal sons who scorn their Mother's house and waste their substance in riotous living, feeding their souls on the husks of sin. Meanwhile their Mother "watches from afar off," praying endlessly for their repentance. If they take one step only toward her, she runs the rest of the way to meet them. The grace of repentance, which Jesus won for sinners, is given to them through Mary.   *Fr. Payton's Rosary Prayer Book*

All the sins of your life seem to be rising up against you. Don't give up hope! On the contrary, call your holy mother Mary, with the faith and abandonment of a child. She will bring peace to your soul.

Josemaria Escriva de Balaguer

We are all children of Eve according to the flesh, and of the Virgin according to the spirit. She has for all the love of a mother and the courage of a defender. See how great she must be to be the Mother of so many children. Just as well as sinners, all find room in her: sinners find pardon through her prayers, and the just are preserved in grace.

If He who is larger than heaven and earth, could find room in her, do you think you sinner will not be able to find room in her? Mary is roomier than the earth. Just and sinners alike find entrance into her. God entered into her and abides in her.   **St. John of Avila**

Mary, compassionate mother
and refuge of sinners,
you know my trials and sorrows.
Present my needs to the Father

and come to my aid in the battle.
Draw me ever nearer to Jesus your Son.
Through Christ our Lord. Amen.

Mary Wages Spiritual Warfare for Us

When warfare blusters at high Lucifer's command,
And writhing monsters fume a course from
    Acheron's land,
With speed of wind and wing, O loving Mother
    haste!
Shield for the plagued of soul,
Sword for the heart laid waste!
Crush with thy virgin foot these cobras of the night,
Erect thy son a tower on the Mary-height
Where he may watch the serpents leave,
As stars in flight. **"War Cry: to Mary" by Pope Leo XIII
(from the Latin by Raymond F. Roseliep)**

*Mary is an incomparable warrior in our spiritual bat-
tles as only a mother can be. In the animal kingdom, no
one fights more fiercely than a mother when the lives of her
offspring are endangered. How much more will Mary
fight to defend us for whom her Son's very blood was shed.
She knows our foe only too well: it is her Son who crushed
the serpent's head. We can rely on Mary's powerful intercession to counter the work of the evil one in our lives, and
in the lives of those we love.*

I will put enmity between you and the woman, and between your seed and her seed; he shall bruise your head, and you shall bruise his heel.   **Genesis 3:15**

Mary is at the very heart of the spiritual warfare which rages against the prince of darkness and the father of lies, the one who opposes the woman and her offspring.   **Pope John Paul II**

And a great portent appeared in heaven, a woman clothed with the sun, with the moon under her feet, and on her head a crown of twelve stars; she was with child and she cried out in her pangs of birth, in anguish for delivery.

And another portent appeared in heaven; behold, a great red dragon, with seven heads and ten horns, and seven diadems upon his heads. His tail swept down a third of the stars of heaven, and cast them to the earth. And the dragon stood before the woman who was about to bear a child, that he might devour her child when she brought it forth; she brought forth a male child, one who is to rule all the nations with a rod of iron, but her child was caught up to God and to his throne, and the woman fled into the wilderness, where she has a place prepared by God.

Revelation 12:1-6

As wax melts before fire, so do the devils lose their power against those souls who remember the name of Mary and devoutly invoke it.   **St. Bonaventure**

In Mary, there is not only an absence of sin, perfect subordination of body to soul and of soul to God, a crystalline purity. But between her and sin there is an open warfare, an active incompatibility. It is she who, by virtue of her office, crushes Satan beneath her feet and untiringly defeats his works of darkness.

She is the light which puts the darkness to flight, the brightness which breaks up the shadows, and thwarts the most cunning of plots.... Directly I unite myself to her, I feel myself at once called to live in union with her holy dispositions, with her exquisite delicacy of soul, with her revulsion from sin and her reaction against the slightest evil.

Cardinal Léon Joseph Suenens

You are an invincible warrior in defense of your servants, fighting against the devils who assail them.

St. Bernard

On earth, Mary, you were all *mother*—infinitely tender, understanding, compassionate. In heaven, while you are our Mother still, you are much more. When the Church sings of you: "Fair art thou, and comely, daughter of Jerusalem," she adds this thunderous refrain: "and terrible as an army set for the fray!"

The gentle, humble Mother of Jesus, sword in hand! What do you make war upon, Mary? The Church tells me: "Rejoice, Mary Virgin! Thou alone hast destroyed all the world's heresies!" It is against Satan, sin, and unbelief that Mary leads the army of

God. Mary is meek, but Mary is mighty. Communism is bound in the coils of her Rosary.

Fr. Payton's Rosary Prayer Book

Freed of sin, Mary is not weaker but the stronger in the fight; and the war she wages with Satan is the war of God and for the souls of men. In the battle with temptation she is from the beginning the leader giving strength, begetting courage. She was never subject to Satan and from her we know we need not be. In her we know our lot; with her we cast our lot with God.   **Ferrer Smith, O.P.**

Mary is present at all the battles we fight for the cause of God, just as a mother who passionately seeks her children's welfare, and is more concerned with it than they are themselves. She sustains their courage, makes good their deficiencies, and seeks to make the light and warmth of Christ penetrate everywhere, so impatient is her love to open to him the way as soon as she finds the instruments.

Cardinal Léon Joseph Suenens

It was revealed to me that through the intercession of the Mother of God all heresies will disappear. The victory over heresies has been reserved by Christ for His Blessed Mother. In the latter days, the Lord will in a special manner spread the renown of His Mother. Mary began salvation, and by her intercession it will be completed.

Before the second coming of Christ, Mary, more than ever, must shine in mercy, might, and grace in order to bring unbelievers into the Catholic faith. The power of Mary in the latter days will be very conspicuous. Mary will extend the reign of Christ over the heathens and the Mohammedans, and it will be a time of great joy when Mary is enthroned as Mistress and Queen of Hearts.   **Blessed Mary of Agreda**

Mary, compassionate mother
and refuge of sinners,
you know my trials and sorrows.
Present my needs to the Father
and come to my aid in the battle.
Draw me ever nearer to Jesus your Son.
Through Christ our Lord. Amen.

FIVE

A Mother's Work Is Never Done

God wants to communicate grace and mercy, love and compassion to the human race. What better vehicle than the mother to whom his Son has entrusted us? Mary is one of God's main messengers, a fountain of his goodness, and a broad channel of his grace and mercy. This is what is meant when we refer to Mary as the Mediatrix of All Graces: she has been especially entrusted with directing the Son's mercy and grace to us. In fact, Pope John Paul II is fond of referring to her as the Mediatrix of Mercy.

While Mary as the Mediatrix of All Graces is not a defined doctrine of the church, it has been the ordinary teaching of the popes for the last one hundred fifty years and has a basis in Scripture and tradition. We have already considered Mary's role at pivotal stages of salvation history: as the New Eve (Genesis

3:15); as the mother of the redeemer who would share uniquely in her Son's sufferings (Luke 2:35); as the spiritual mother of the redeemed (John 19:26-27); and as the woman who is in the forefront of the spiritual warfare until her Son comes again (Revelation 12). These Scriptures and numerous references to Mary in various church documents clearly demonstrate her special role in God's work of redemption.

Mary's role as the channel of all graces wholly depends on the merits of Christ as the Universal Mediator and flows from God as the source of all grace. While herself completely dependent on the grace of God, Mary's unparalleled love and friendship with God enables her to plead as the Queen of Heaven on our behalf. Mary cares for her children who are surrounded by dangers and difficulties by distributing God's graces to those in need. A mother never forgets her children. Mary hears our every cry, and indeed is sent by the Son to surround us with his love and mercy even before we call.

A Channel of Grace and Mercy

I say that we are wound
With mercy round and round
As if with air: the same

Is Mary, more by name.
She, wild web, wondrous robe,
Mantles the guilty globe,
Since God has let dispense
Her prayers his providence:
Nay, more than almoner,
The sweet alms' self is her
And men are meant to share
Her life as life does air.
**"The Blessed Virgin
Compared to the Air We Breath"
by Gerard Manley Hopkins**

God sends to us the one who personifies his love: Mary, the spouse of the Spirit—a spirit of maternal love—immaculate, all beautiful, spotless, even though she is our sister, a true daughter of the human race. God confides to her the communication of his mercy to souls. He makes of her the Mediatrix of the graces merited for us by her divine Son, for she is full of grace, the mother of all souls born of grace, reborn, and always being reborn, becoming ever more Godlike. **St. Maximilian Kolbe**

Her Son is our Mediator (1 John 2:1); she, our Mediatrix—but in a very different manner, as I have said a hundred times. The Savior is the Mediator of justice, for He intercedes for us, exposing the right and reason of our cause. He produces our just claims, which are none other than His Redemption, His Blood, His Cross. He acknowledges to His Father that we are debtors, but He shows that He has paid for us.

But the Virgin and the saints are mediators of grace. They pray for us that we may be pardoned—all through the mediation of the Passion of the Savior. They themselves have nothing to show by which we may be justified, but entrust themselves to the Savior for this. In brief, they do not join their prayers to the intercession of the Savior, for they are not of the same quality, but to ours.

If Jesus Christ prays in Heaven, He prays in virtue of Himself; but the Virgin prays only as we do, in virtue of her Son, but with more credit and favor. Do you not see that all returns to the honor of her Son and magnifies His glory? **St. Francis de Sales**

The Heart of this good Mother is all love and mercy. She desires only to see us happy. We have only to turn to her to be heard. **St. John Vianney**

No doubt, we must not exaggerate or indulge in any excess as regards this devotion to Mary. We must especially avoid anything that might suggest equality of Mary with Almighty God such as making her the source of grace. As long, however, as we see in her but a creature possessed of no grandeur, no holiness, no power save such as her Creator bestowed upon her, there can be no danger of sinning by excess. It is then God Himself whom we honor and venerate in her. **Adolphe Tanquerey**

We praise her virginity, we admire her humility; but because we are poor sinners, mercy attracts us more and tastes sweeter; we embrace mercy more lovingly; we remember it more often, and invoke it more earnestly. **St. Bernard**

Mary, then, is the one who has the deepest knowledge of the mystery of God's mercy. She knows its price; she knows how great it is. In this sense, we call her the Mother of Mercy, Our Lady of Mercy or Mother of Divine Mercy....

It was precisely this "merciful" love, which is manifested above all in contact with moral and physical evil, that the heart of her who was the Mother of the Crucified and Risen One shared in singularly and exceptionally—that Mary shared in. In her and through her this love continued to be revealed in the history of the church and of humanity.

This revelation is especially fruitful because in the Mother of God it is based upon the unique tact of her maternal heart, on her particular sensitivity, on her particular fitness to reach all those who most easily accept the merciful love of a mother. This is one of the great life-giving mysteries of Christianity, a mystery intimately connected with the mystery of the incarnation. **Pope John Paul II,** *Redemptoris Mater*

Mary is, as it were, the heavenly canal by which the waters of all graces and gifts flow down into the souls of wretched human beings. **Pope Benedict XIV**

Jesus is King of the eternal ages by nature and by conquest; through Him, with Him, and subordinate to Him, Mary is Queen by grace, by divine kinship, by conquest, and by singular choice. And her domain is as vast as that of her Son and God, for nothing is exempt from her dominion.   **Pope Pius XII**

Among living mortals you are a living spring of hope. Lady, you are so great and have such worth, that if anyone seeks out grace and flies not to you, his longing is like flight without wings. You help not only those who ask, but often freely give your kind solace without request. In you is mercy and pity, in you is lavishness, in you is all the goodness that is possible in created things.   **Dante Alighieri**

The nineteen centuries which have elapsed since the day of Her glorious Assumption seem to bow under the gentle weight of Her acts of generosity. Her charity has indeed overflowed throughout the centuries, as She never ceased showering innumerable spiritual and material graces.

    She does not limit Her acts of kindness to Her faithful children: She continually extends them also to Her prodigal children. Thus She shows Herself to be always the Mother of Mercy. The supreme goal of Mary's ongoing, uninterrupted action for all Her children, whether good or bad, is none but their salvation.... She is, and acts as, Mother of all. Mary has and can have but one single irresistible desire: to see all Her children in Heaven with Her, close to Her Motherly Heart.   **Gabriel M. Roschini, O.S.M.**

Your name, O Mary, is a precious ointment, which breathes forth the odor of Divine grace. Let this ointment of salvation enter the inmost recesses of our souls.   **St. Ambrose**

> *Hail Mary, full of grace,*
> *help me to receive more of God's grace.*
> *Help me to know more of God's mercy,*
> *more of my Father's love and compassion.*
> *Help me to give my life more fully to God,*
> *to live in daily repentance and prayer.*
> *Through Christ our Lord. Amen.*

A Messenger of God's Love and Compassion

O Lady, together with the Child you take
In your frail arms to hush His frightened cries,
Cradle us against your heart and ache
To see the sorrow staring from our eyes.
O Lady strong beyond all ecstasy,
Young willow bent before the Breath of God,
Think still of us as little ones while we
Thrust puny chests at Heaven from this sod
And flail with futile fists against the Breast
Where beats the Beauty passion cannot taste.

O Lady, heal our wars, our dark unrest,
The lusts that lash our land a scarlet waste:
Mother of men, this bleeding face
Awaits the wonder of your love's embrace.

**"Cry from the Battlefield"
by Robert Menth**

God's love is beyond our ability to comprehend, and so he tells us again and again, "I love you." Mary is a special messenger of God's love and compassion, closely entwined with her role as a channel of grace and mercy. God is love. Mary knows the love of God as no other human being. She longs to help us grab hold of this truth, so that we may receive life itself from the source of life. Listen to your mother and receive her embrace, and so receive the love of God.

In this work of progressive transformation, Mary is not a late appendage dreamed up by the Christian piety of later centuries. She is an instrument of the Holy Spirit from the very beginning, not merely in the birthing and human formation of Jesus but in the spiritual formation of the church. The Holy Spirit surely uses other instruments—the Word of God, the preaching of the church, the sacraments. But in the Holy Spirit's quiver of tools, there is none more powerful than the example of the saints, and here the mother of Jesus has the primordial place. She is not a metaphor but a revealing symbol in person. She exemplifies total surrender to the plan of God, a surrender that is not passivity but activation of all her powers. She is not a symbol for the subjugation of women to men; she is the symbol of the submission of every Christian and of the church as a whole to God. And though not divine, she mediates the maternal love and consolation of God, fulfilling that function prophesied for mother Jerusalem (Isaiah 66:13). **George Montague, S.M.**

The Lord himself created Wisdom; he saw her and apportioned her, he poured her out upon all his works. She dwells with all flesh according to his gift, and he supplied her to those who love him…. Those who serve her will minister to the Holy One; the Lord loves those who love her….

"I am the mother of beautiful love, of fear, of knowledge, and of holy hope; being eternal, I am therefore given to all my children, to those who are named by him. Come to me, you who desire me, and eat your fill of my produce."

Book of Sirach 1:9-10; 4:14; 24:18-19

Mary is a most sweet bait that God has prepared to catch the hearts of men. **St. Catherine of Siena**

After the humanity of Christ, Mary is God's supreme attempt to convince us of His love. She has nothing that she did not receive from Him. After the human nature of Christ she is the crowning point of His creation. He is the source of all her love and all her care for us. In Mary God loves us with a love that seems to come within the order of things felt by our hearts. Mary is… an unequalled introduction to the knowledge of the love of God. **Cardinal Léon Joseph Suenens**

Mary is so endowed with feelings of compassion, that she not only deserves to be called merciful, but even mercy itself. **Pope St. Leo the Great**

In order to shine out clearly, this light-bringing spiritual dawn came to dwell in the radiance of the Sun of Righteousness, in obedience to him who rose by his own power to give light to all creation. Through her the splendor that outshines even the rays of the sun sheds his light upon us in mercy and compassion, stirring up in the souls of believers the desire to imitate as far as they can his divine kindness and goodness. **St. Modestus**

Even when the Mother of God lived in this valley of tears, she was inexpressibly loving and merciful toward the afflicted; how much more compassionate is she now since she reigns happily in Heaven! Now she realizes human misery more fully, and therefore manifests her mercy and assistance more generously. **St. Bonaventure**

All that belongs to Mary is filled with grace and mercy, for she, as a Mother of mercy, has made herself all to all, and out of her most abundant charity she has made herself a debtor to the wise and the foolish, to the just and sinners, and opens to all her compassionate heart, that all may receive of the fulness of its treasures.　**St. Bernard**

Since Mary is Jesus' gift to us, she relates us immediately to him as giver of the gift and as our elder brother. That is easily seen. What is less often perceived is that Mary's maternal love and influence is not a complement or balance to the Father's love. Even less is it the "back door of mercy" in contrast to the "front door of justice" (a homiletical trick that is a theological absurdity). Her love is rather the *instrument of God's own maternal love,* which was only implicit in the biblical term "Father" but is clearly and beautifully mediated in a unique way through Mary. She is not a metaphorical appendage but a revelation in person of the maternal face of God. There is nothing Mary has that she has not received. Her maternal love is first of all God's love for us.

George Montague, S.M.

Once we have found Mary we may find Jesus through her. Through Jesus we can find the Father. Hence, through Mary, we shall find all good—all good without exception, all grace, all love, all truth, all comfort, all joy, all courage, all safety from the enemies of God.

It does not follow that one who has found Mary

will be exempt from the carrying of crosses. On the contrary, he will be blessed with more sufferings than are given others! Mary gives her children portions of the Tree of Life, which is the cross of Jesus, [but also helps her loved ones] to carry their crosses patiently, even cheerfully. The crosses she lays on those belonging to her are redolent of sweetness.

St. Louis de Montfort

> *Hail Mary, full of grace,*
> *help me to receive more of God's grace.*
> *Help me to know more of God's mercy,*
> *more of my Father's love and compassion.*
> *Help me to give my life more fully to God,*
> *to live in daily repentance and prayer.*
> *Through Christ our Lord. Amen.*

Marian Apparitions

Hail, queen of the heavens,
    Hail, mistress of earth,
Hail, virgin most pure,
    Of immaculate birth:

Clear star of the morning,
    In beauty enshrined,
O Lady, make speed
    To the help of mankind! **Hail, Holy Queen**

Mary's efforts to communicate God's grace and mercy have been manifested in the repeated visitations of Our Lady from her heavenly home to earth. These apparitions have prompted some to call our times the "Marian age." Again and again, Mary has intervened to warn the human race that we are in grave danger. We will take a brief look at just three of the Marian apparitions which have received church approval: Guadalupe (1531); Lourdes (1858); and Fatima (1917).

Mary's appearances share some striking similarities. First, she does not come to the wealthy or learned among us, but rather to the poorest, humblest, most unlearned of her children—to those who would receive her message simply and without question. Second, her message is always the same: Mary calls us to repent of our disobedience to God, to return to a life of prayer and penance, a life of faith and love. Third, to convince us of God's love and mercy, Mary brings his healing to many.

Out of her motherly love and concern for her children, Our Lady comes to warn and to plead. She warns that God's judgment cannot be held off much longer. She pleads with us to accept the salvation offered by her Son Jesus before it is too late. She portrays the anguish and sorrow of a mother who sees her children going down a treacherous path that surely leads to death.

Mary comes particularly for the conversion of sinners. Through Mary's intercession, Christ can move the most hardened of hearts. Listen to her message from God in these visitations, and be renewed in your zeal to love the Lord your God with all your heart, mind, and soul.

It is Mary's prerogative to be the *Morning Star*, which heralds in the sun. She does not shine for herself, or from herself, but she is the reflection of her and our Redeemer, and she glorifies *Him*. When she appears in the darkness, we know that He is close at hand.

Cardinal John Henry Newman

There were varied physical phenomena associated with the different apparitions of Our Lady, but the most spectacular of all was a part of every one of these appearances. Without exception, Our Lady's appearances were accompanied by brilliant light— light of an unearthly intensity but which despite its brilliance did not hurt the eyes of those experiencing the vision. In the Fatima apparition, when Francisco was being questioned about the brightness of the Virgin, he was asked, "Which was brighter, the fig- ure of the Virgin or the sun?" The answer was, "The figure of the Virgin was brighter." And of course it was at Fatima that the sun performed its terrifying dance.

At Guadalupe, Juan Diego speaks of the golden beams that rayed her from head to foot. St. Catherine Labouré says the angel who led her to the chapel "was surrounded with rays of light" and when describing Our Lady exclaims at "the beauty and the brilliance of the dazzling rays" that encompassed her. And so it was with every visitation. Brilliant, dazzling light of an unearthly quality bathed Mary in its rays.   **John J. Delaney**

One of the many ways by which Mary fulfills her role as Mother of all is by lovingly manifesting herself to chosen witnesses, usually innocent, simple children who typify those who enter the kingdom of her Son (cf. Matthew 18:3). Her message is always an insistence upon the Gospel proclamation as lived, taught, and prayed by the Church. Her purpose is always to center us on her Son, the "one Mediator between God and man, the man Christ Jesus" (1 Timothy 2:5).   **Catherine Odell**

If we examine the content of the seven universally acclaimed apparitions of Mary which have taken place in our own times we are bound to see how the ancient treasure of Christianity is simply related in these apparitions to the spiritual needs of our own situation. Mary confirms our sinfulness and the fact of Christ's redemption and urges us to prayer and repentance. The circumstances in which this confirmation takes place, however, all point to the charismatic element of divine inspiration, by means of which God seeks to activate this ancient treasure of Christian life in our own times.

Edward Schillebeeckx, O.P.

The apparitions of Mary seem to continue this generosity of a God who often bolstered belief by touching men where and when they needed it. They seem to be perceivable examples of the giving nature of which Mary, next to her Son, is the purest example. That goodness that visionaries saw on her face is her motivation to come.

"The Lady looked at everyone and with so much love and affection," Bernadette said, following one of the later apparitions. "Sometimes she seemed to be looking one by one at the people there, and now and again her look would rest on someone for a moment as though she had recognized a friend." **Catherine Odell**

The Blessed Virgin Mary, Mother of God, Mother of Sorrows, does not come to take away the Cross of Christ, but rather to give it. She came to Lourdes in 1858 to heal the sick, and since then she has healed thousands whose cures scientific medicine cannot explain; but the majority who come to Lourdes are not healed, but go back to home or hospital to bear their cross anew, to suffer and die.

She came to Fatima in 1917 during the First World War in response to Pope Benedict XV's anguished prayers for peace, for an end to the horrible and pointless slaughter of that war; she asked for more prayers for peace, and finally announced that peace would come—only to be followed by another, still greater war and by the advance of a great new evil out of Russia to spread all over the world.

When she came to Tepeyac in 1531 after the conquest of Mexico, she brought about the conversion of its people; but that conversion has been followed by much oppression and persecution.   **Warren H. Carroll**

> *Hail Mary, full of grace,*
> *help me to receive more of God's grace.*
> *Help me to know more of God's mercy,*
> *more of my Father's love and compassion.*
> *Help me to give my life more fully to God,*
> *to live in daily repentance and prayer.*
> *Through Christ our Lord. Amen.*

Our Lady of Fatima

At morn, at noon, at twilight dim,
Maria, thou hast heard my hymn:
In joy and woe, in good and ill,
Mother of God, be with me still.
When the hours flew brightly by,
And not a cloud obscured the sky,
My soul, lest it should truant be,
Thy grace did guide to thine and thee.
Now, when storms of fate o'ercast
Darkly my present and my past,
Let my future radiant shine
With sweet hopes of thee and thine.
"Hymn" by Edgar Allan Poe

The world was in the midst of a brutal and bloody war in 1917, and the situation in Europe especially looked hopeless. In this hour of darkness and rebellion, in May, the month of Mary, the Mother of God appeared to three illiterate shepherd children in Portugal. She promised that if humanity heeded her pleas for peace and penitence, the war would come to an end. If not, an even more devastat-ing war would come to pass.

While playing with Jacinta and Francisco on the hill-top in the Cova da Iria, making a little stone wall around a furze-like clump called *moita*, suddenly we saw a flash as of lightning.

"There is a flash of lightning," I said to my cousins. "A thunderstorm may come on, it would be better for us to go home."

"Oh yes, of course," they said. And we began to descend the hill driving the sheep along towards the road. When we reached a large holm-oak about half way down the slope the light flashed again. Then a few paces further on, we beheld a beautiful lady dressed in white, poised over a holm-oak sapling very near us. She was more brilliant than the sun, radiating a sparkling light.

Struck with amazement, we halted before this vision. We were so near that we were bathed in the light that radiated from Her person to a distance of about three feet. Then the Lady said: "Do not be afraid, I will do you no harm."

"Where are you from?" I asked.
"I am from Heaven." **Sister Lucia of Fatima**

Lucia then asked the Lady if she would take the three of them to heaven. This time, the answer was more specific. The Lady promised to take Francisco and Jacinta to heaven with her soon. But for Lucia, there was a different plan. She was to remain on earth longer to help establish worldwide devotion to the Lady's Immaculate Heart.

"I stay here alone?" Lucia asked with sadness.

The woman answered her with great tenderness. She would never really be alone, Lucia was told. "My Immaculate Heart will be your refuge." With that, the woman extended her hands. Great showers of light seemed to pour forth as before, but one shaft seemed to flow down upon Lucia. The other radiated back up to the sky from the sister and brother. All three saw a vision of the Immaculate Heart.

Catherine Odell

It was in anticipation of this global insurrection against God that the Blessed Virgin interceded with her Divine Son to permit the frightening reality of Hell to be shown to the world for a searing instant. We read in the parable of Dives and Lazarus that God refused to show Hell to the world, explaining that its existence must be accepted through faith. That Our Lady obtained the grace of this vision seems like the action of a broken-hearted Mother seeing great numbers of her children in dire peril of being cast into eternal fire. **Francis Johnston**

"You see hell, where the souls of poor sinners go." she said at length. "To save them God wishes to establish in the world the devotion to my Immaculate Heart. If they do what I will tell you, many souls will be saved and there will be peace. The war is going to end. But if they do not stop offending God, another and worse one will begin in the reign of Pius XI.

"When you shall see a night illuminated by an unknown light, know that it is the great sign that God gives you that He is going to punish the world for its crimes by means of war, of hunger, and of persecution of the Church and of the Holy Father.

"To prevent this I come to ask the consecration of Russia to my Immaculate Heart and the Communion of reparation on the First Saturdays. If they listen to my requests, Russia will be converted and there will be peace. If not she will scatter her errors through the world, provoking wars and persecution of the Church. The good will be [martyred], the Holy Father will have much to suffer, various nations will be annihilated.

"In the end my Immaculate Heart will triumph. The Holy Father will consecrate Russia to me, and it will be converted and a certain time of peace will be granted to the world." **William Thomas Walsh**

Yet despite these ominous portents, it would be wrong to view Fatima in an exclusively foreboding light. The great promise of the ultimate triumph of the Kingdom of God is a dazzling sign of hope for a tormented and fearful world. By this wondrous pledge, God manifests His unwearying love and concern for His wayward children. Though much of the world had abandoned Him, He has not abandoned the world.

He reveals Himself through His Mother and promises to withhold the terrible arm of His justice and forgive His rebellious sons. If a "sufficient number" correspond with His grace and return to His waiting arms like the Prodigal Son, He assures us of final reconciliation and peace. But having given us free wills, He expects us to correspond with the grace of His message to attain that consummation so devoutly to be wished without having to be purified through suffering. **Francis Johnston**

The crowds watched in awe as the sun bobbed in the sky like a bright silver top. Then the "dancing sun" stopped and began to spin. As it whirled, bright rays representing every color of the spectrum shot off and washed everything on the earth. Green, red, violet worlds appeared momentarily to surround the people, who shouted and praised God.

Then seventy thousand there at the Cova watched the sun plunge in a zigzag path toward the earth. In every heart there was a fear of death. People fell to their knees by the hundreds. Just as the sun seemed about to strike the earth, it stopped and was suddenly returned to its proper place and its proper brightness. The crowd noticed that all clothing, previously soaked with rain, had dried. The "Miracle of the Sun" was seen in nearby cities. There was no serious talk of mass hallucination. Portugal was convinced.

Catherine Odell

The apparitions of Our Lady at Fatima are an eloquent expression for our times of the role the Virgin Mary fulfills in the mystery of the Word Incarnate and of the Mystical Body. She is the messenger from Heaven who points the way to Jesus Christ, the only way, the truth, and the life. She is the motherly heart who offers refuge to her children, to lead them to God by prayer and by penance. She is the cry of supplication who begs of men not to offend God anymore, for He is already too greatly offended. The Virgin of Fatima is, after all, the Virgin of Nazareth, of Bethlehem, of Cana, of Galilee, of Calvary, and of Pentecost, ever eager to give Christ to the world and the world to Christ.

Cardinal Patriarch Antonio Ribeiro of Lisbon

While the message of Our Lady of Fatima is a motherly one, it is also strong and decisive. It sounds severe. It sounds like John the Baptist speaking on the banks of the Jordan. It invites to repentance. It gives a warning. It calls to prayer. It recommends the rosary.

The message is addressed to every human being. The love of the Saviour's mother reaches every place touched by the work of salvation. Her care extends to every individual of our time and to all the societies, nations, and people—societies menaced by apostasy, threatened by moral degradation.

Joseph A. Pelletier, A.A.

On May 13, 1982, Pope John Paul II traveled to Fatima to consecrate the world to the Immaculate Heart of Mary in collegial union with the bishops of the church. Exactly one year before, he had survived an assassination attempt—which he believed was due to Mary's protection. The following is part of this prayer of consecration:

And therefore, O Mother of individuals and peoples, you who know all their sufferings and their hopes, you who have a mother's awareness of all the struggles between good and evil, between light and darkness, which afflict the modern world, accept the cry which we, as though moved by the Holy Spirit, address directly to your Heart. Embrace with the love of a mother and handmaid this human world of ours, which we entrust and consecrate to you, for we are full of disquiet for the earthly and eternal destiny of individuals and peoples.

In a special way we entrust and consecrate to you those individuals and nations which particularly need to be entrusted and consecrated.

We have recourse to your protection, holy Mother

of God. Reject not the prayers we send up to you in our necessities.

Reject them not!

Accept our humble trust—our act of entrusting!

... The power of this consecration lasts for all time and embraces all individuals, peoples, and nations. It overcomes every evil that the spirit of darkness is able to awaken and has in fact awakened in our time and in the heart of man and in his history.

Pope John Paul II

Hail Mary, full of grace,
help me to receive more of God's grace.
Help me to know more of God's mercy,
more of my Father's love and compassion.
Help me to give my life more fully to God,
to live in daily repentance and prayer.
Through Christ our Lord. Amen.

Our Lady of Lourdes

She has put on the chasuble of the sun, and her
     stole of stars, and she takes the horns of the
     slender moon for her candelabrum,
And she walks in the way of the Light of the
     world, the sick lie in wait for her passing,
For she brings our daily bread and the oil that
     anoints all fevered foreheads.
The balm of all pierced hearts and the chrism for
     all our fears,

And she bears sweet charities like a seamless
    garment,
Full of lilies of the field and of five-for-a-farthing
    sparrows,
Down forbidden alleys and over flat hills by paths
    forgotten,
And the urn of living water by which death is
    immortality,
Closing eyes like the eyes of Joseph:
Jesus, Mary, and Joseph, assist me in my last agony.
May I breathe forth my soul in peace, with you.

                        "The Mediatrix of Grace"
                                    by Francis Burke

In 1858, in a remote grotto in the French foothills of the Pyrenees, Mary appeared to Bernadette Soubirous, "a poor, sickly, uneducated peasant girl" of fourteen. Bernadette had come to gather firewood for her cold and hungry family. Our Lady spoke to her in the local dialect, asking her to come to the grotto for fifteen days. During that time, Mary revealed an awesome truth to Bernadette: "I am the Immaculate Conception."

Since the revolt against God [The Enlightenment] was led by such brilliant men, we might expect Mary to combat it by raising up a saint of great intellectual powers—a saint who would lead people back to God by the very brilliance of his arguments. Instead, Mary chose Bernadette Soubirous, a poor, sickly, uneducated peasant girl, who at the age of fourteen did not even know her catechism.   **Don Sharkey**

When Bernadette first went to the grotto of Massabielle, which has now become world famous, it was without the slightest inkling that anything extraordinary, much less miraculous, was about to happen. She went because she and all her family, including her little brothers and sisters, were cold and hungry, and there was nothing in the hovel where they lived which would supply fuel for warmth and cooking; and the trip was one which involved hardship and even some danger. Her reward for persisting in this hazardous undertaking was overwhelming, not only to her personally, but to the whole world.

John J. Delaney

"I had just begun to take off my first stocking when suddenly I heard a great noise like the sound of a storm. I looked to the right, to the left, under the trees of the river, but nothing moved; I thought I was mistaken. I went on taking off my shoes and stockings; then I heard a fresh noise like the first. I was frightened and stood straight up. I lost all power of speech and thought when, turning my head toward the grotto, I saw at one of the openings of the rock a rosebush, one only, moving as if it were very windy.

"Almost at the same time there came out of the interior of the grotto a golden-colored cloud, and soon after a Lady, young and beautiful, exceedingly beautiful, the like of whom I had never seen, came and placed herself at the entrance of the opening above the rosebush. She looked at me immediately, smiled at me, and signed to me to advance, as if she had been my mother. All fear had left me but I seemed to know no longer where I was."

St. Bernadette Soubirous

For us, the sublimity of the vision is softened by its simplicity. The little girl saw Mary as herself, hardly more than a child: the Vision smiled, talked patois [the local dialect]: was clothed so modestly and without adornment (save for that exquisite detail of the two dawn-colored roses resting on her feet), wholly unlike the blue and crimson heavily-gilt Madonnas of that region.   **F. J. Sheed**

"Would you have the graciousness to come here for fifteen days?" she asked the girl in the local patois. Bernadette agreed instantly with a heart full of warmth. The woman had asked her with such tenderness, such deference, and respect. Then the woman told her: "I do not promise to make you happy in this world but in the next."   **Catherine Odell**

Our Lady revealed a spring of water during the ninth apparition. This water was to become world famous for the miraculous cures worked through it.... The growth of the shrine was rapid after that. Three great churches were built, one above the other, and a hospital for sick pilgrims. Today it is one of the most famous shrines in the world. A million and a half pilgrims go there every year. The devotion of these pilgrims is inspiring. So many people are praying at the same time and with such intensity that the air seems to be charged with prayer.   **Don Sharkey**

Lourdes has simply planted the banner of the Supernatural and of Holiness—of supernatural holiness—in our modern earth. It has proclaimed anew an entirely different *order* of existence, and in that order Mary, conceived immaculate, is, as it were, the perfect unsurpassable example, the peak, the exact reproduction of God's Idea. Need we after all find "I am the Immaculate Conception" to be so strange an expression? Must we think that it would have been impossible for Our Lord to say: "I am the Incarnation"? After all, He did say: "I am the Resurrection and the Life." God's Thought is substantial in Him. God's Vision of Humanity "full of grace" is realized in Mary. She *is* what the bitterly jealous world, the indignant, humiliated, self-worshipping would simply not admit.   **F. J. Sheed**

"Few indeed are those who… are present as eyewitnesses of one of those rare but terribly real occurrences in which the omnipotence of God strikes through the shadows of time and space to bind up and heal the broken bodies of men. But the evidence of these visitations is indisputable. During the last century it has pleased God so to visit His people time after time at a remote grotto in the French foothills of the Pyrenees, where the Blessed Virgin Mother of God appeared in 1858 to little Bernadette Soubirous. God, of course, chooses His own times and places and occasions for the miraculous, but His power shines forth most frequently where His Mother is honored and venerated." ·

The above quotation was taken from an important editorial which appeared in the Catholic weekly *America,* for January 1958. It is important to us, in the present study of a certain saint, for two reasons: it singles out Bernadette Soubirous—a young Bigourdane peasant of sordid background, elementary education, and limited opportunity—as a striking example of the many "lowly and meek" exalted by the Almighty for one of those "rare examples" of occurrences when the omnipotence of God strikes through the shadows of time and space; and it stresses the point that, whereas God chooses His Own times and places and occasions for such miracles, "His power shines forth most frequently where His mother is honored and venerated."   John J. Delaney

Even twenty years after, the apparitions at Lourdes had transformed the area around Massabielle so that Bernadette would have scarcely recognized it. Today, twenty-seven thousand gallons of water are generated from the spring which started with a mudhole that day that Bernadette dug with her fingers. Some three hundred fifty thousand people pass by the grotto each day, and Lourdes has become and remained the most popular healing shrine and pilgrimage site in the world. Five thousand healings have been attributed to the intercession of Our Lady of Lourdes over the years, although the Church admits only sixty-four of them to the category it calls "miraculous." **Catherine Odell**

Madame Bire, in 1908, had her sight restored although her optic nerves were atrophied. Oculists testified that according to all laws of science she was blind. Yet she could read the smallest type in the newspapers.

In 1875, Pierre de Rudder had an inch of bone created instantaneously in his left leg. No law of science can explain this. It happened at a Lourdes shrine in Belgium.

Father McSorley in his book, *Outline of Church History*, says that, in the fifty years following 1858, some four thousand medically miraculous cures were recorded at Lourdes. They are still taking place at the rate of about fifteen per year. **Don Sharkey**

> *Hail Mary, full of grace,*
> *help me to receive more of God's grace.*
> *Help me to know more of God's mercy,*
> *more of my Father's love and compassion.*
> *Help me to give my life more fully to God,*
> *to live in daily repentance and prayer.*
> *Through Christ our Lord. Amen.*

Our Lady of Guadalupe

O Mary, dearest Mother!
　　If thou wouldst have us live,
Say that we are thy children
　　And Jesus will forgive.

Our sins make us unworthy
　　That title still to bear;
But thou art still our Mother
　　Then show a Mother's care.

Open to us thy mantle;
　　There stay we without fear:
What evil can befall us
　　If, Mother, thou art near?　**St. Alphonsus**

In December, 1531, Juan Diego, a poor, simple Aztec Indian only one generation removed from paganism, was making the three-day hike to Mass in Mexico City. Suddenly Mary appeared to him, and asked in his Indian language that a church be built there in her honor. She then asked Juan Diego to deliver her message to the Bishop of Mexico City. When the skeptical bishop asked Juan to come back another time, Mary had Juan gather roses into his rough cloak. Not only was it wintertime—which made any flowers scarce—but roses did not grow in the desert.

When the bishop opened Juan's blanket, all those present saw not only the amazing roses, but the breathtaking image of Mary which had been infused onto the rough cloth—the same image that still hangs in the great Basilica of Guadalupe near Mexico City. As a result of this miracle, eight million Indians were converted to Christianity with in the decade. Mary was later named Patroness of all Latin America and Mother of the Americas.

As Juan approached the crest of Tepeyac Hill, he saw a cloud encircled with a rainbow of colors. Then he heard strange music coming from the hill as well. Could it be from some sort of rare bird? he wondered. He stared up at the hill and the sun now rising behind it. A woman's voice was calling above the music. He was fascinated but confused.

"Juanito, Juan Dieguito..." the voice came, urging him. Since it seemed to be coming from behind the top of the hill, he ascended to the crest to look. A beautiful woman, strikingly beautiful, stood there beckoning him. She radiated such light and joy that Juan Diego could think of nothing more to do than drop to his knees and smile at her. **Catherine Odell**

Speaking to him in his Indian language and cadence she told him that she was the "Immaculate Virgin Mary, Mother of the true God." She expressed her earnest desire that a church be built there and went on to tell him, "Here... I will give all my love, my compassion, my help, and my protection to the people. I am your merciful mother, the merciful mother of all of you who live united in this land, and of all

mankind, of all those who love me, of those who cry to me, of those who seek me, of those who have confidence in me. Here I will hear their weeping, their sorrows, and will remedy and alleviate their many sufferings." Gerald J. Farrell, M.M.
and George W. Kosicki, C.S.B.

There was a pause. He could see the love and sympathy flowing from the Lady's steadfast gaze, and the tenderness of her gentle response moved him almost to tears. "Listen and let it penetrate your heart, my dear little son," she said consolingly, in words that were to echo down the centuries, moving millions of her children to throw themselves into her comforting arms.

"Do not be troubled or weighed down with grief. Do not fear any illness or vexation, anxiety or pain. Am I not here who am your Mother? Are you not under my shadow and protection? Am I not your fountain of life? Are you not in the folds of my mantle? In the crossing of my arms? Is there anything else you need?" She paused, smiling at him, and then added, "Do not let the illness of your uncle worry you because he is not going to die of his sickness. At this very moment, he is cured."

In these sublime words, uttered to a humble Mexican peasant, Our Lady disclosed to all her suffering children the exquisite tenderness of her Immaculate Heart. Her words are a personal message of deep love and maternal solicitude destined for each one of us, regardless of our creed, our color, our race, or our class. The glorious Mother of God had come to the barren hill of Tepeyac, later to become the site of a vast and world-famous shrine, as the compassionate Mother of all mankind, the Mother of pity and of grace, the Mother of mercy to whom Our Lord in His hour of extreme agony on the cross entrusted us, in order that, as He intercedes with His Heavenly Father for us, she may likewise intercede with her Son on our behalf. **Francis Johnston**

Then she told Juan Diego to climb up the hill, saying that he would find flowers blooming there which he should pluck and bring to her. The hill was a desert place where only cactus, thistles, and thornbush grew. Juan Diego had never seen a flower there. But when he reached the top, it was covered with beautiful Castilian roses, touched with dew, of exquisite fragrance. Mary took them from him as he gathered them, arranged them with her own hands, and put them in his cloak, or *tilma*, made of the fiber of the maguey cactus, and tied a knot in it behind his neck to hold the roses in place. **Warren H. Carroll**

When he arrived again at the Bishop's house Juan Diego was kept waiting a long time by the Bishop's attendants, who eventually insisted on seeing the roses; but when they tried to take some of them they could not, because they became "not roses that they touched, but were as if painted or embroidered."

When they finally admitted him to the Bishop's presence, Juan Diego told him all that had happened, and opened his cloak. The roses cascaded to the floor; and there upon the *tilma* was a full portrait of the Mother of God, in Indian dress, her small hands joined in prayer, her soft black hair falling gently upon her shoulders under her cape and framing the perfect oval of her face, with half-closed eyes deep as the sea, and the rosebud mouth, slightly smiling, that had kissed the Infant God on Christmas Day in Bethlehem.   **Warren H. Carroll**

The seer saw the Blessed Virgin as a person of his own race, and was firm in his conviction. Her physiognomy in the painting bears him out, as also do her garments. Her star-studded outer mantle resembles that of an Aztec queen. In so appearing she showed herself a mother to him and to his people in a most special way; but the picture's expression is archetypical of adorable motherhood in every race of man.

John J. Delaney

As part of the celebration, the Indians reenacted a mock battle by the lake near Tepeyac Hill. In the excitement, one of the Indians was accidently pierced with an arrow in the neck. He died near the feet of the bishop and others escorting the precious *tilma*.

With grief, but with faith too, he was picked up and placed in front of the mounted image of Our

Lady of Guadalupe. Within moments, the "dead" man sat up. The arrow was carefully withdrawn, with no apparent damage except for a scar where the arrow had entered. Tepeyac Hill went wild with joy. Spaniards and the Aztecs, recently released from the horror of a pagan cult, had discovered a living Mother who cared for her children.   **Catherine Odell**

In perhaps the greatest crisis in Mexican history after the conquest itself, when the revolutionary constitution of 1917 (the year Mary appeared at Fatima) had turned over full control of the Church in Mexico to the bitterly anti-Catholic government of Obregon and Calles, the Church's enemies struck at Our Lady of Guadalupe directly. A bomb was concealed in a bouquet of flowers placed under her sacred image on November 14, 1921. It exploded during Mass. Pieces of stone were ripped from the sanctuary; the force of the explosion twisted a heavy metal cross on the altar into an almost circular shape. But not one worshipper in the packed church was hurt; and the sacred image was absolutely untouched.

Warren H. Carroll

The *tilma* of Juan Diego comprises two straight lengths of ayate fiber sewn together in the center and woven so coarsely that when viewed close-up it appears to be almost transparent.... The lifespan of the ayate fiber is approximately twenty years. Yet after four hundred and fifty years, the *tilma* still shows not the slightest sign of decay. Its colors remain as vivid and fresh as when they first materialized before Bishop Zumarraga's astounded gaze. And this despite the fact that for over a century the sacred image hung unprotected even by glass in a damp, open-windowed chapel the size of an average living room, where it was directly exposed to ceaseless smoke and incense, burnt perfumes, and the myriads of votive candles flickering beneath it.

Francis Johnston

It was a sublime experience to gaze on the silent splendor of the sacred image. The Lady's features, ineffably delicate, were those of a beautiful girl, of olive complexion, with rosy cheeks and dark brown hair. The eyes, cast down in an attitude of humility, were so full of expression that they seemed more like those of a living being. She wore a rose-colored garment overlaid with a fine lace-like sheath worked with an exquisite floral design of gold. A greenish-blue mantle covered her head and fell to her feet. The glowing beauty of her person, together with an indefinable aura of a supernatural presence, has captivated untold millions down to this day.   Francis Johnston

Hail Mary, full of grace,
help me to receive more of God's grace.
Help me to know more of God's mercy,
more of my Father's love and compassion.
Help me to give my life more fully to God,
to live in daily repentance and prayer.
Through Christ our Lord. Amen.

Part Two

A Selection of
Marian Prayers

SIX

Cries of the Heart

Throughout the centuries, Christians have cried out to Mary for mercy and protection. Especially when we come face to face with our own weakness, our sin, our insufficiency, we naturally long for a mother's warm and loving embrace from which we can draw strength and courage.

As our loving mother, Mary is always there for us—interceding for us at the feet of her Son. As the Spouse of the Holy Spirit, Mary is always there for us—bringing us closer to the heart of God. As our ally in spiritual warfare, Mary is always there for us—strengthening us in the battles of faith.

Perhaps you will recognize some of the cries of your own heart in the following prayers. Let us begin by invoking the Holy Spirit, who alone can reveal to us our heavenly Father. Humbly we ask the Holy Spirit to unite us with Mary so that with her, like her, and in her, we can enter more fully into the life of Jesus.

211

MOST HOLY SPIRIT,
>   Help us to relive,
>   in union with Mary, the joyful,
>   sorrowful and glorious mysteries of Jesus.
> Grant that we may be
>   —inspired by the faith of our Baptism,
>   —nourished by the Eucharist,
>   —renewed in the grace of Pentecost.
> So as to live,
>   —in word and deed,
>   —always and everywhere,
>   —as faithful witnesses of Christ and of
>   —the love of His Divine Heart. Amen.

"The FIAT Prayer"
by Cardinal Léon Joseph Suenens

Modern Prayers

Although beautiful and powerful, some of the traditional Marian prayers can be less familiar in terminology and spirituality. Here is a selection of prayers from more recent times which capture cries of the heart typical of modern-day life.

Mary, you know I've had a hard time identifying with you, seeing you as a real person. I've tried lots of different things, lots of times—prayers, devotions, rosaries—but nothing has worked. I feel like there is a barrier between us that can't be broken. You're too holy for me to relate to.   **Mary Lee Bensman**

It is good to examine your humanness, Mary. But tonight I got an overwhelming sense of trying to dethrone you. I felt a great sadness at trying to wrench you from your magnificent place in heaven and in my life. I felt embarrassed at trying to funnel you into my own weaknesses in an attempt to demystify you. But you are mysterious. You are human, but holy. You are humble, yet exalted. You are a woman, but the Mother of God....

I see, now, that there is more to you than just your humanity. I'm beginning to reembrace those beliefs I once discarded. In seeking you, I'm finding knowledge, wisdom, and understanding that you are, indeed, all those things I was taught but couldn't comprehend. I'll never fully comprehend now, but I can begin to reaccept—to embrace more fully, more deeply.

Forgive me for staying away so long.

Mary Lee Bensman

The will of God led Jesus through the terrible suffering of Calvary. The will of God led you to watch his suffering. You were not supposed to carry his cross. You were busy with your own cross of a pierced heart. How badly you must have wanted to rescue your Son from the will of God.

Yet, as you had surrendered and accepted his conception, you also accepted his death. You said yes to his entering your life in a personal, intimate way. In

doing that, you also said yes to the heartache and
pain. This has got to be one of the hardest lessons for
me to learn, Mary—to sit powerlessly by while someone I love walks in pain and suffering.

Mary Lee Bensman

Mary, help me to believe that you are my Mother,
that Jesus intended you for me at Cana and Calvary.
Let me place my need to be healed in your hands,
confident that your loving Son will hear your
    request.
Lead me to the Christ who gives water from the well
    of life
to all who thirst. Amen.   **Gloria Hutchinson**

Mary, you call us forth
from the darkness of unknowing and affliction.
You call us into faith and fruitful caring.
Lead us on, never letting us forget
the hand waiting to be taken,
the Jesus-face longing to be seen. Amen.

Gloria Hutchinson

Mother, will I remember that faith requires me
to forsake the pretense of self-sufficiency
and remove the prickly garment of impatience?
Will I embrace the human heritage
of insecurity and unanswered questions,
of waiting like a well-disposed child
for the Father's word?

Shall I bruise my knees with pleading
and turn my back on the one who cannot kneel?
No, not if you are with me,
not if you refuse to let me go,
not if you require of me faith
that does justice to its name. Amen.   **Gloria Hutchinson**

Give us a heart as beautiful, pure, and spotless as
yours. A heart like yours, so full of love and humility.
May we be able to receive Jesus as the Bread of Life,
to love him as you loved him, to serve him under the
mistreated face of the poor. We ask this through Jesus
Christ our Lord. Amen.   **Mother Teresa of Calcutta**

Come, Mother of the Lord, visit me! Let your greeting sound in my ears, and I, like Elizabeth, will be
filled with joy in the Holy Spirit! "Let me see your
face, let me hear your voice, for your voice is sweet,
and your face is comely!" (Song of Songs 2:14).
                                        Paul Hinnebusch, O.P.

O Mother Mary, teach me to be a home, have a home,
but do not let me be content to cling to my abode in
the land of exile in which I dwell with comforts.
Teach me to find my home as an orphan and
    stranger among orphans and strangers.
Teach me not to fear the journey,
I who always make sure that I have reservations at
    an inn with clean sheets (cow dung and sheep out
    of sight!)

whenever I do venture forth from home;
I who would despise the aid of a rough carpenter or
the praise of silly shepherds—I turn to the people
   who "count":
—and do not count myself among the huddled mass-
es who get counted by the Divine Augustuses.

O Seat of Wisdom, I ask you:
   Help me not to be afraid of angel voices singing
      praise,
    · of dark birthing caves and of the poverty within
      them;
    · of rough helping hands;
    · of clashing opposites within and without my-
      self;
    · of mother love that weaves a seamless garment
      of comfort from womb to tomb;
    · of carrying Jesus wherever I go;
    · of being a home to myself and for others.
You refuge of sinners, ark of the covenant, seat of
   wisdom! **Mary Neill**

Still another privilege of yours, Mary, makes me feel
very little beside you. I reflect how often I've refused
to follow the invitations of God's grace; how often,
perhaps, I've even fallen from the state of grace, living to repent only by God's sheerest mercy.

   Then I remember how different you were—full of
grace!

   Full of grace at your Immaculate Conception;
filled with a new fullness at the Incarnation, at the

Nativity, on Calvary, at Pentecost, at your death; and at every moment of your life, growing beyond belief in the loving friendship of God. As a forest fire is to a flickering taper, so is your sanctity compared to that of all saints and angels combined.

Hail Mary, full of grace! Pray for us sinners.

Fr. Payton's Rosary Prayer Book

Virgin, model of every virtue, I kneel at your feet, filled with shame at my coldness and ingratitude. Pray to Jesus for me that He will never come to my heart without directing all its movements and turning them entirely to Himself. May He take away this wretched heart of mine that is so unworthy of Him and create in me a new heart. May He give me a heart like yours: ardent and generous, tender and constant toward Him, as yours now is toward us.

Alexander de Rouville

Virgin, spouse of the Holy Spirit, obtain for me the spirit of wisdom, so that I may taste the riches of heaven and find tasteless all the deceitful goods and empty riches of this world.

Obtain for me the spirit of understanding and light, that I may be enlightened here in this realm of darkness and come to know the ways of God and the truths of eternity.

Obtain for me the spirit of discernment and counsel, that I may discover and avoid the snares which the enemies of salvation and perfection have laid for me.

Obtain for me the spirit of strength and courage

that will raise me above my weakness, enable me to overcome my passions, resist the world's vanity, and strengthen myself against my own inconstant heart.

Obtain for me the spirit of piety and fear of the Lord that will guide and inspire me in His service, in the observance of His law, and in the worship I owe Him as my creator, father, savior, and judge.

Alexander de Rouville

O Mary, we have exiled your Divine Son from our lives, our councils, our education, and our families! Come with the light of the sun as the symbol of His Power! Heal our wars, our dark unrest; cool the cannon's lips so hot with war! Take our minds off the atom and our souls out of the muck of nature! Give us rebirth in your Divine Son, us, the poor children of the earth grown old with age! **Fulton J. Sheen**

It is the time for your Visitation. Arise, Mary, and go forth in your strength into that north country, which once was your own, and take possession of a land which knows you not. Arise, Mother of God, and with your thrilling voice, speak to those who labor with child, and are in pain, till the babe of grace leaps within them! **Cardinal John Henry Newman**

O Mary conceived without sin, pray for us who have recourse to you. You have been so closely associated with the whole work of our redemption, associated with the cross of our Savior. Your heart was pierced by it, beside his heart. And now, in the glory of your Son, you do not cease to intercede for us, poor sinners.

You watch over the Church and are the mother of the Church. You watch over each of your children. You obtain for us from God all those graces symbolized by the rays of light emanating from your open hands. The sole condition on our part is that we come to you with confidence, with boldness, and with the simplicity of a child.

Day by Day With Our Daily Visitor

Your work is done,
You can leave your Cross,
You can come down to rest, you have surely earned
    it.

Slowly you slip down, like a man weary of labor and
    drowsy with sleep.
Your mother takes you in her arms. You rest in peace.
Over your face, calm and serene, there passes a ray
    of joy. All is accomplished.
You have made your mother suffer, but she is proud
    of you.
"Sleep now, my little one, your Mother is watching
    you."

Thus each night, my day ended, I fall asleep.
What a state I am in sometimes, Lord.

But, alas, it is not always in serving the Father that I
    have become soiled and tired.
Mary, will you be willing, even so, to watch over me
    every night?
My body is weighed down with its failures, but my
    heart asks forgiveness.
Don't forget, you are the refuge of sinners.

Holy Mary, Mother of God, pray for me, a poor
    sinner.
Grant that through the merits of your Son, I may
    never fall asleep without receiving the forgiveness
        of our Father,
That, each night, resting in peace in your arms,
    I may learn how to die.   **Michel Quoist**

Short Prayers to Mary

*One of my favorite prayers to my heavenly Father is:
"O God!" or just plain "HELP!" Sometimes, these short
and to the point prayers seem to capture our immediate
and heart-felt distress and helplessness. In the same way,
we do not always need to recite long, involved prayers to
our spiritual mother. Mary is always glad to hear from us,
even if it's just a simple "Hello, I'm glad you're here."
Here is a collection of short prayers which may be helpful
at times in expressing the cries of your heart.*

Mary, I love you.

Mary, make me live in God, with God, and for God.

Draw me after you, holy mother.

O Mary, may your children persevere in loving you.

Mary, Mother of God and mother of mercy, pray for me and for the departed.

Mary, holy Mother of God, be our helper.

In every difficulty and distress, come to our aid, O Mary.

O Queen of Heaven, lead us to eternal life with God.

Mother of God, remember me, and help me always to remember you.

O Mary, conceived without sin,
pray for us who have recourse to you.

Pray for us, O holy Mother of God,
that we may be made worthy of the promises of Christ.

Holy Mary, Mother of God, pray to Jesus for me.

St. Philip Neri

Open to us the gate of mercy, O holy Mother of God!

St. John Damascene

Grant me, O Mary, that I may get to know the cross; not only Jesus' cross, but whatever cross fits me best.

St. Gemma

O Mary, may my heart never cease to love you, and my tongue never cease to praise you.

St. Bonaventure

O Lady, by the love which you bear Jesus, help me to love him.   **St. Bridget**

O, that the soul of Mary were in us to glorify the Lord!
That the spirit of Mary were in us to rejoice in God.

St. Ambrose

Prayers of the Saints

Like Mary, the saints often seem too holy, out of reach of common sinners. But these were men and women of flesh like you and me who loved God with pure hearts and often understood the love and care of Mary in a very clear way. The church means for them to be living examples to us of holiness. Even though these prayers were uttered centuries ago, they still beautifully capture the cries of the heart of any age.

Virgin Mary, hear my prayer: through the Holy Spirit you became the Mother of Jesus; from the Holy Spirit may I too have Jesus. Through the Holy Spirit your flesh conceived Jesus; through the same Spirit may my soul receive Jesus. Through the Holy Spirit you were able to know Jesus, to possess Jesus, and to bring him into the world. Through the Holy Spirit may I too come to know your Jesus.

Imbued with the Spirit, Mary, you could say: "I am the handmaid of the Lord, be it done unto me according to your word"; in the Holy Spirit, lowly as I am, let me proclaim the great truths about Jesus. In the Spirit you now adore Jesus as Lord and look on him as Son; in the same spirit, Mary, let me love your Jesus. **St. Ildephonsus of Spain**

Have mercy on me, O Lady, for my enemies have trodden upon me every day: all their thoughts are turned to evil against me. Stir up fury, and be mindful of war: and pour out your anger upon them. Renew wonders and change marvellous things: let us feel the help of your arm. Distill upon us the drops of your sweetness: For you are the cupbearer of the sweetness of grace. **St. Bonaventure**

O my Mother, you who always burned with love for God, deign to give me at least a spark of it. You prayed to your Son for those spouses who were lacking wine, saying: *"They have no more wine!,"* and will you not pray for me, so lacking as I am in the love of God, whereas I am so very obliged to love Him? Say, if you will: *"He has no love!"* And ask this love for me.

O Mother, for the love you bear Jesus, hear me. Show me how great is the grace you possess before Him, by asking for me a light and a divine flame so powerful that it will transform me from a sinner into a saint, and that, detaching myself from all earthly affection, I will become wholly inflamed by divine love. Do it, O Mary, for you can do it; do it for love of that God Who made you so great, so powerful, and so merciful. Amen.   St. Alphonsus

To you we cry, O Queen of Mercy! Return, that we may behold you dispensing favors, bestowing remedies, giving strength.... Ah, tender Mother! Tell your all-powerful Son that we have no more wine. We are thirsty after the wine of his love, of that marvelous wine that fills souls with a holy inebriation, inflames them, and gives them the strength to despise the things of this world and to seek with ardor heavenly goods.   St. Bernard

Run, hasten, O Lady, and in your mercy help your sinful servant, who calls upon you, and deliver him from the hands of the enemy. Who will not sigh to you? We sigh with love and grief, for we are oppressed on every side. How can we do otherwise than sigh to you, O solace of the miserable, refuge of outcasts, ransom of captives? We are certain that when you see our miseries, your compassion will hasten to relieve us.

O our sovereign Lady and our Advocate, commend us to your Son. Grant, O blessed one, by the grace which you have merited, that he who through you was graciously pleased to become a partaker of our infirmity and misery, may also through your intercession, make us partakers of his happiness and glory. **St. Bernard**

Jesus entrusted me to his Mother, and charged me to love her very much. You are then my heavenly Mother. You will be towards me like any mother towards her children. You see me weak? You will have mercy on my weakness. You see me poor in virtue? You will help me. O my Mother, do not forsake me! My dearest Mother, do not abandon me!
                                                    St. Gemma

Mary, I beg you, by that grace through which the Lord is with you and you will to be with him, let your mercy be with me. Let love for you always be with me, and the care for me be always with you. Let the cry of my need, as long as it persists, be with you, and the care of your goodness, as long as I need it, be with me. Let joy in your blessedness be always with me, and compassion for my wretchedness, where I need it, be with you. **St. Anselm**

O, Mother of my God, and my Lady Mary; as a beggar, all wounded and sore, presents himself before a great Queen, so do I present myself before you, who are Queen of heaven and earth. From the lofty throne on which you sit, disdain not, I implore you, to cast your eyes on me, a poor sinner. God has made you so rich that you might assist the poor, and has made you Queen of Mercy in order that you might relieve the miserable. Behold me then, and pity me: behold me and abandon me not, until you see me changed from a sinner into a saint.   St. Alphonsus

O Immaculate and wholly-pure Virgin Mary, Mother of God, Queen of the world, hope of those who are in despair: You are the joy of the saints; you are the peacemaker between sinners and God; you are the advocate of the abandoned, the secure haven of those who are on the sea of the world; you are the consolation of the world, the ransom of slaves, the comfortress of the afflicted.…

O great Queen, we take refuge in your protection. After God, you are all my hope. We bear the name of your servants; allow not the enemy to drag us to hell. I salute you, O great mediatress of peace between men and God, Mother of Jesus our Lord, who is the love of all men and of God, to whom be honor and benediction with the Father and the Holy Ghost. Amen.   St. Ephrem

Hail, O Mother! Virgin, heaven, throne, glory of our Church, its foundation and ornament. Earnestly pray for us to Jesus, your Son and Our Lord, that through your intercession we may have mercy on the day of judgment. Pray that we may receive all those good things which are reserved for those who love God. Through the grace and favor of Our Lord, Jesus Christ, to whom, with the Father and the Holy Spirit, be power, honor, and glory, now and forever. Amen.

St. John Chrysostom

O Mary, I give you my heart. Grant me to be always yours. Jesus and Mary, be ever my friends; and, for love of you, grant me to die a thousand deaths rather than to have the misfortune of committing a single mortal sin. **St. Dominic Savio**

By you we have access to your Son, O blessed finder of grace, Mother of Life, Mother of Salvation, that by you He may receive us, Who by you was given to us.

St. Bernard

Papal Prayers

As Vicar of Christ, the pope is charged with the care of the people of God. Papal prayers are often expressed as part of a public gathering and give voice to our corporate inter-cession for world peace, for nations, for families, and for children. The following selection offers a glimpse into the hearts of a few popes through their cries to Mary.

Mary, show that you are our Mother; may our prayer be heard by that Jesus who willed to be your Son.

Pope Leo XIII

Look down with maternal clemency, most Blessed Virgin, upon all your children. Consider the anxiety of bishops who fear that their flocks will be tormented by a terrible storm of evils. Heed the anguish of so many people, fathers and mothers of families who are uncertain about their future and beset by hardships and cares. Soothe the minds of those at war and inspire them with "thoughts of peace." Through your intercession, may God, the avenger of injuries, turn to mercy. May He give back to nations the tranquility they seek and bring them to a lasting age of genuine prosperity. **Pope Paul XI**

O Mary, you are praying for us, you are always praying for us. We know it, we feel it. Oh what joy and truth, what sublime glory, in this heavenly and human interchange of sentiments, words and actions, which the rosary always brings us: the tempering of our human afflictions, the foretaste of the peace that is not of this world, the hope of eternal life!

Pope John XXIII

O Mary, your name has been on my lips and in my heart from my early infancy. When I was a child I learned to love you as a Mother, turn to you in danger, and trust your intercession. You see in my heart the desire to know the truth, to practice virtue, to be prudent and just, strong and patient, a brother to all.

O Mary, help me to keep to my purpose of living as a faithful disciple of Jesus, for the building up of the Christian society and the joy of the holy Catholic Church. I greet you, Mother, morning and evening; I pray to you as I go upon my way; from you I hope for the inspiration and encouragement that will enable me to fulfill the sacred promises of my earthly vocation, give glory to God, and win eternal salvation. O Mary! Like you in Bethlehem and on Golgotha, I too wish to stay always close to Jesus. He is the eternal King of all ages and all peoples. Amen.

Pope John XXIII

Show us that you are our Mother, even if we so little deserve this motherly love. But a mother's love is always greater! In it is manifested the mercy of God himself, which is more powerful than every evil that has taken possession of man's history and his heart. You who, treading on the serpent's head, embrace the whole world in your Immaculate Heart, show that you are a Mother! Amen. **Pope John Paul II**

Be with us more and more. Meet us more and more often, because we need it so much. Speak to us by your motherhood, by your simplicity and holiness. Speak to us by your Immaculate Conception! Speak to us continually! And obtain for us the grace—even if we are distant—of not becoming insensitive to your presence in our midst. Amen.   **Pope John Paul II**

Accept us! Look into our hearts! Accept our concerns and our hopes! *Help us,* you who are full of grace, to live in grace, to persevere in grace, and, if necessary, to return to the grace of the living God, which is man's greatest and supernatural good.

Prepare us for your Son's coming! Accept us! With our everyday problems, our weaknesses and deficiencies, our crises, and personal, family and social shortcomings. Do not let us lose goodwill! Do not let us lose sincerity of conscience and uprightness of behavior! With your prayer, obtain justice for us. Safeguard peace in the whole world!

In a short time we shall all leave this place. We wish, however, to return to our homes with this joyful certainty that you are with us, you, Mary Immaculate, you, chosen for centuries to be Mother of the Redeemer. Be with us. Be with Rome. Be with the Church and with the world. Amen.   **Pope John Paul II**

Mother of the Church, grant that the Church may enjoy freedom and peace in fulfilling her saving mission and that to this end she may become mature with a *new maturity* of faith and inner unity. Help us to overcome opposition and difficulties. Help us to rediscover all the simplicity and dignity of the Christian vocation. Grant that there may be no lack of "laborers in the Lord's vineyard."

Sanctify families. Watch over the souls of the young and the hearts of the children. Help us to overcome the great moral threats against the fundamental spheres of life and love. Obtain for us the grace to be continually renewed through all the beauty of witness given to the cross and resurrection of your Son. Amen.   **Pope John Paul II**

Mother, I commend and entrust to you all that goes to make up earthly progress, asking that it should not be one-sided, but that it should create conditions for the full spiritual advancement of individuals, families, communities, and nations.

I commend to you the poor, the suffering, the sick and the handicapped, the aging, and the dying. I ask you to reconcile those in sin, to heal those in pain, and to uplift those who have lost their hope and joy. Show to those who struggle in doubt the light of Christ your Son. Amen.   **Pope John Paul II**

Prayers for Home and Nation

Prayer to Mary, Queen of the Home

O Blessed Virgin Mary, you are the Mother and Queen of every Christian family. When you conceived and gave birth to Jesus, human motherhood reached its greatest achievement. From the time of the Annunciation you were the living chalice of the Son of God made Man.

You are the Queen of the home. As a woman of faith, you inspire all mothers to transmit faith to their children. Watch over our families. Let the children learn free and loving obedience inspired by your obedience to God.

Let parents learn dedication and selflessness based on your unselfish attitude. Let all families honor you and remain devoted to you, so that they may be held together by your example and intercessions. Amen.   **Alexander de Rouville**

Prayer for the Conversion of a Nation

O blessed Virgin Mary, Mother of God, and our most gentle queen and mother, look down in mercy upon our nation, and upon us all who greatly hope and trust in you. By you it was that Jesus, our Savior and our hope, was given to the world. He has given you to us that we might hope still more.

Plead for us your children, whom you did receive and accept at the foot of the cross, O sorrowful mother. Intercede for our separated brothers and sisters, that with us in the one true fold, they may be united to the chief shepherd, the vicar of your Son.

Pray for us all, dear mother, that by faith fruitful in good works, we may all deserve to see and praise

God, together with you, in our heavenly home.
Amen. **The Catholic Prayer Book**

Prayers of Marian Dedication or Consecration to Mary

As a way to enter into a fuller union with Mary, many have found it helpful to make a specific act of dedication or consecration. Pope John Paul II states that reading St. Louis de Montfort's True Devotion to Mary *marked a decisive turning point in his life. In fact, his Marian motto* Totus Tuus *comes from this saint.*

By entrusting to our spiritual mother everything we have and do, we trust that Mary will make our love and service of God more fruitful than otherwise possible. The following prayers can be used to actively accept God's gift of Mary as our mother, and thereby allow God to conse - crate us more fully to himself.

Lord Jesus,
To the disciple whom you loved
You gave Mary, your Mother,
As your final gift before you died,
That she should be his mother and mine.
As the beloved disciple took her to be his own,
So I now take her as my mother.
Under her influence may I be formed
By the Holy Spirit to your likeness
And proclaim the gift you continue to make of her

For the building up of your body, the church,
To the glory of God the Father. Amen.

George Montague, S.M.

Mary, Mother of Jesus and Mother of Mercy,
   since Jesus from the Cross gave you to me,
   I take you as my own.
And since Jesus gave me to you, take me as your
   own.
Make me docile like Jesus on the Cross,
   obedient to the Father, trusting in humility and in
   love.
Mary, my Mother, in imitation of the Father,
   who gave his Son to you, I too give my all to you:
   to you I entrust all that I am, and all that I have
   and all that I do.
Help me to surrender ever more fully to the Spirit.
Lead me deeper into the Mystery of the Cross, the
   Cenacle, and the fullness of Church.
As you formed the heart of Jesus by the Spirit, form
my heart to be the throne of Jesus in his glorious
coming. Amen.   **Gerald J. Farrell, M.M.**
                and George W. Kosicki, C.S.B.

Virgin full of goodness, Mother of mercy,
I entrust to you my body and my soul, my thoughts
   and my actions, my life and my death.
O my Queen, come to my aid and deliver me from
   the snares of the devil.
Obtain for me the grace of loving my Lord Jesus

Christ, your Son, with a true and perfect love, and after Him, O Mary, of loving you with all my heart and above all things. Amen.   **Alexander de Rouville**

SEVEN

Prayers through the Centuries

A wealth of prayers and devotions have flourished through the centuries as ways to call upon Mary. They have lost none of their power to draw us closer to our spiritual mother. This treasury of traditional prayers and hymns can serve as a resource. Perhaps you will discover afresh in them the love and strength of Mary.

The best known of traditional prayers and devotions is the Hail Mary and the rosary. An integral part of Catholic devotional practice since before the thirteenth century, the rosary recalls the principal mysteries of our salvation in three groups of five decades. Many popes have been dedicated to Mary and found great power in praying the rosary in particular.

The Hail Mary and the Holy Rosary

The Hail Mary

Hail Mary, full of grace,
the Lord is with you!
Blessed are you among women,
and blessed is the fruit of your womb, Jesus.
Holy Mary, Mother of God,
pray for us sinners,
now and at the hour of our death.

The Holy Rosary

Introductory Prayers
    The Sign of the Cross
    The Apostles' Creed
    One Our Father
    Three Hail Marys
    One Glory Be

The Decades
    Announce the First Mystery
    One Our Father
    Ten Hail Marys
    One Glory Be
    Fatima Prayers
    (follow this sequence for the remaining decades)

Concluding Prayers
    Hail, Holy Queen

Let us pray: O God, whose only-begotten Son, by his life, death, and resurrection has purchased for us the rewards of eternal salvation, grant, we beseech you, that meditating upon these mysteries in the most holy rosary of the Blessed Virgin Mary, we may both imitate what they contain and obtain what they promise, through the same Christ our Lord. Amen.

Optional: The Litany of the Blessed Virgin Mary

The Mysteries of the Rosary

The Joyful Mysteries (usually said on Mondays and Thursdays throughout the year and on Sundays from Advent to the beginning of Lent)

1. *The Annunciation* (Luke 1:28-38)
   Mary, Jesus will be your Son. Teach me to love him.
2. *The Visitation* (Luke 1:32-45)
   Mary, you visit your cousin, Elizabeth. Help me to be kind.
3. *The Nativity* (Luke 2:6-7)
   Jesus, you are born in a stable. May I value grace above money.
4. *The Presentation of Jesus* (Luke 2:22-24)
   Jesus, you are offered to God in the temple. Help me to obey.
5. *The Finding of Jesus in the Temple* (Luke 2:46-52)
   Jesus, you are found with the teachers. Give me true wisdom.

The Sorrowful Mysteries (usually said on Tuesdays and Fridays and on Sundays during Lent)

1. *The Agony of Jesus in the Garden* (Mark 14:32-36)
   Jesus, you are saddened by my sins. Give me true sorrow.
2. *The Scourging at the Pillar* (John 19:1)
   Jesus, you are whipped by the soldiers. Help me to be pure.
3. *The Crowning with Thorns* (John 19:2)
   Jesus, you receive a crown of thorns. Give me true courage.
4. *The Carrying of the Cross* (John 19:17)
   Jesus, you carry the cross gladly. Help me to be patient.
5. *The Crucifixion* (Luke 23:33, 44-46)
   Jesus, you die on the cross for me. Keep me in your grace.

The Glorious Mysteries (usually said on Wednesdays, Saturdays, and also on Sundays from Easter to Advent)

1. *The Resurrection of Jesus* (Matthew 28:5-6)
   Jesus, you rise from your tomb. Help me to believe in you.
2. *The Ascension of Jesus into Heaven* (Acts 1:6-12)
   Jesus, you go to your Father in heaven. Help me to hope in you.
3. *The Descent of the Holy Spirit* (Acts 2:1-4)

Holy Spirit, you come to bring grace. Help me to love God.

4. *The Assumption of Mary into Heaven* (Revelation 12:1)

   Mary, you are taken to heaven. Let me be devoted to you.

5. *The Coronation of Mary* (Revelation 12:1)

   Mary, you are crowned Queen of Heaven. Let me serve you.

Hail, Holy Queen (Salve Regina)

Hail, holy Queen, Mother of mercy; hail, our life, our sweetness, and our hope. To you we cry, poor banished children of Eve; to you we send up our sighs, mourning, and weeping in this land of exile. Turn then, most gracious advocate, your eyes of mercy toward us; lead us home at last and show us the blessed fruit of your womb, Jesus; O clement, O loving, O sweet Virgin Mary. Pray for us, O holy Mother of God, that we may be made worthy of the promises of Christ.

The Fatima Prayers

These prayers were taught to Lucia, Jacinta, and Francisco by the angel who preceded Mary's appearance at Fatima, with the request that they be said with the rosary.

O my Jesus, forgive us our sins, save us from the fires of hell. Lead all souls to heaven, especially those in most need of your mercy.

O Jesus, it is for your love, for the conversion of sinners, and in reparation for the sins committed against the Immaculate Heart of Mary [when offering a penance].

My God, I believe, I adore, I hope, and I love you. I ask pardon for those who do not believe, do not adore, do not hope, and do not love you.

Traditional Prayers and Hymns to Our Lady

A wealth of traditional Marian prayers and hymns have been used throughout the centuries. Individuals often develop their own particular devotion to our Lady under one of her various titles.

The Angelus

The angel of the Lord declared unto Mary:
And she conceived of the Holy Spirit. Hail Mary…

Behold the handmaid of the Lord:
Be it done unto me according to your word. Hail Mary…

And the Word was made flesh:
And dwelt among us. Hail Mary…

Pray for us, O holy mother of God,
That we may be made worthy of the promises of Christ.

Let us pray. Pour forth, we beseech you, O Lord,

your grace into our hearts, that as we have known the incarnation of Christ, your Son, by the message of an angel, so by his passion and cross we may be brought to the glory of his resurrection, through the same Christ our Lord. *Amen.*

We Fly to Your Patronage

We fly to your patronage, O holy Mother of God. Despise not our petitions in our necessities, but deliver us always from all dangers, O glorious and blessed Virgin.

Memorare

Remember, most loving Virgin Mary, never was it heard that anyone who turned to you for help was left unaided. Inspired by this confidence, though burdened by my sins, I run to your protection for you are my mother. Mother of the Word of God, do not despise my words of pleading but be merciful and hear my prayer. Amen.   St. Bernard

Queen of Heaven (Regina Coeli)

O Queen of heaven, rejoice! Alleluia.
For the Son you merited to bear, alleluia,
has risen as he said, alleluia.
Pray to God for us, alleluia.
Rejoice and be glad, O Virgin Mary, alleluia.

For the Lord has risen indeed, alleluia.

Let us pray: God of life, you have given joy to the world through the resurrection of your Son, our Lord Jesus Christ. Through the prayers of his mother, the Virgin Mary, bring us to the happiness of eternal life. We ask this through Christ our Lord. Amen.

Tota Pulchra

You are all fair, O Mary, the original stain is not in you. You are the glory of Jerusalem, you are the joy of Israel, you are the honor of our people, you are the advocate of sinners. O Mary, Virgin most prudent, Mother most merciful, pray for us, intercede for us with our Lord Jesus Christ.

Holy Mary, Help the Helpless

Holy Mary, help the helpless, strengthen the fearful, comfort the sorrowful, pray for the people, plead for the clergy, intercede for all women consecrated to God; may all those who honor your memory experience your generous help.

Remember, O Most Gracious Virgin Mary

Remember, O most gracious Virgin Mary, that never was it known that anyone who fled to your protection, implored your help or sought your intercession was left unaided. Inspired with this confidence, I fly to you, O Virgin of virgins, my Mother; to you do I come, before you I stand, sinful and sorrowful. O Mother of the Word Incarnate, despise not my petitions, but in your mercy hear and answer me.

Ave Maria of the Seven Sorrows

Hail Mary, full of sorrow, Jesus crucified is with you! You are deserving of pity among all women, and Jesus, the fruit of your womb, is worthy of all compassion. Holy Mary, Mother of my suffering Jesus, obtain for us sinners, who have crucified your Divine Son, tears of repentance and love, now and at the hour of our death. Amen.

Anima Mariae

Soul of Mary, sanctify me.
Heart of Mary, inflame me.
Hands of Mary, support me.
Feet of Mary, direct me.
Immaculate eyes of Mary, look upon me.
Lips of Mary, speak for me.
Sorrows of Mary, strengthen me.
O Mary, hear me.
In the wound of the Heart of Jesus, hide me.
Let me never be separated from you.
From my enemy defend me.
At the hour of my death call me,
And bid me come to your Immaculate Heart;
That thus I may come to the Heart of Jesus,

And there with the saints praise you
For all eternity. Amen.

Ave, Maris Stella

Hail, bright star of ocean,
God's own Mother blest,
Ever sinless Virgin,
Gate of heavenly rest.

Taking that sweet Ave
Which from Gabriel came,
Peace confirm within us,
Changing Eve's name.

Break the captive's fetters,
Light on blindness pour,
All our ills expelling,
Every bliss implore.

Show thyself a Mother;
May the Word Divine,
Born for us thy Infant,
Hear our prayers through thine.

Alma Redemptoris Mater

Mother of Christ! Hear thou thy people's cry,
Star of the deep, and Portal of the sky!

Mother of Him who thee from nothing made,
Sinking we strive, and call to thee for aid.

Oh, by that joy which Gabriel brought to thee,
Thou Virgin first and last, let us thy mercy see.

Our Lady of Good Counsel

Most glorious Virgin, chosen by the eternal counsel
to be the mother of the eternal Word made flesh, treasure of divine grace, and advocate of sinners, I, the
most unworthy of your servants, beseech you to be
my guide and counselor in this valley of tears.
Obtain for me by the most precious blood of your
Son, the pardon of my sins, the salvation of my soul,
and the means necessary to obtain it. Grant that the
holy Catholic Church may triumph over the enemies
of the gospel, and that the kingdom of Christ may be
propagated on earth.

Our Lady of Perpetual Help

Most holy Virgin Mary, who, to inspire me with
boundless confidence, has been pleased to take that
name, Mother of Perpetual Help, I beseech you to
aid me at all times and in all places; in my temptations, in my difficulties, in all the miseries of life, and,
above all, at the hour of my death, so that I may
share in the resurrection of your Son, our Lord Jesus
Christ.

Grant most charitable mother, that I may remember you at all times, and always have recourse to you; for I am sure that if I am faithful in invoking you, you will promptly come to my aid. Obtain for me, therefore, the grace to pray to you unceasingly with filial confidence, and that, by virtue of this constant prayer, I may obtain your perpetual help and persevere in the practice of my faith.

Bless me most tender mother, ever ready to aid me, and pray for me now and at the hour of my death. Mother of Perpetual Help, protect also all those whom I recommend to you, the Church, the Holy Father, our country, my family, my friends and enemies, especially all those who suffer.

Our Lady of Fatima

O most holy Virgin Mary, Queen of the most holy rosary, you were pleased to appear to the children of Fatima and reveal a glorious message. We implore you, inspire in our hearts a fervent love for the recitation of the rosary. By meditating on the mysteries of the redemption, may we obtain the graces and virtues that we ask, through the merits of Jesus Christ, our Lord and Redeemer.

Our Lady of Lourdes

O Immaculate Virgin Mary, you are the refuge of sinners, the health of the sick, and the comfort of the afflicted. By your appearances at the Grotto of Lourdes you made it a privileged sanctuary where your favors are given to people streaming to it from the whole world. Over the years countless sufferers have obtained the cure of their infirmities—whether of soul, mind, or body. Therefore I come with limitless confidence to implore your motherly intercessions. Loving mother, obtain the grant of my requests. Let me strive to imitate your virtues on earth so that I may one day share your glory in heaven.

Our Lady of Guadalupe

Our Lady of Guadalupe, mystical rose, intercede for the Church, protect the holy Father, help all who invoke you in their necessities. Since you are the ever Virgin Mary and Mother of the true God, obtain for us from your most holy Son the grace of a firm faith and a sure hope amid the bitterness of life, as well as an ardent love and the precious gift of final perseverance.

Prayers for the Major Marian Feast Days

One of the traditional ways that Mary is honored in the church is through special feast days. Following are prayers which I have composed for each occasion to help you to celebrate the special gift of a spiritual mother. Although they are not centuries old, these prayers will hopefully serve to strengthen your appreciation of Mary on these important feast days and stimulate your own prayer life with Mary.

The Solemnity of Mary, Mother of God
(January 1)

Hail Mary! You are full of grace! Betrothed to the carpenter, Joseph, you became the Mother of God. A humble virgin, you were privileged to be the mother of the Son of God. You were chosen from among all women to be so highly honored. We honor you, mother and model of all the church. We celebrate your motherhood and rejoice in the gift of a mother's love. Bring Jesus to birth in a waiting and hungry world. Intercede for us, O Holy Mother of God.

The Feast of the Presentation of the Lord
(February 2)

Hail Mary! You are full of grace! You were obedient to God in every way, the obedient mother who presented her Son at the temple. You listened for God's word regarding your child and pondered it in your heart. You did not hold back even when the words were difficult, but persevered in your motherly duties. Teach us to persevere through difficulties, always pondering the Word of God and clinging to the love of God. Intercede for us, O Holy Mother of God.

The Solemnity of the Annunciation of the Lord
(March 25)

Hail Mary! You are full of grace! You are the hand-maid of the Lord who has found favor with God. You received the angel's message in faith, conceived the Son of God in your womb by the power of the Holy Spirit, and bore him in purest love. You are blessed because you believed the word of the Lord and hoped in his promises. You are the yes of all mankind to the mystery of salvation. We honor you as the mother of Jesus, the ark of the new covenant. Intercede for us, O Holy Mother of God.

The Feast of the Visitation
(May 31)

Hail Mary! You are full of grace! We greet you with Elizabeth: blessed are you among women, and blessed is the fruit of your womb, Jesus. You were blest because you believed the promises of God, because you listened to God's word and put it into practice. You were blessed because of your persever-ance, your simple life, your motherly faithfulness, your steadfast prayer. We honor you because you were perfect in love of God and neighbor. We rejoice in your example of humble service. Intercede for us, O Holy Mother of God.

The Solemnity of the Assumption
(August 15)

Hail Mary! You are full of grace! We rejoice that you were carried body and soul to the glory of heaven. You who stood at the foot of the cross now make your home in the bridal chambers of heaven. We behold you, the fulfillment of the hopes of all humanity. You are the sign of the hope of heaven for all of us who are destined for glory. Adorned with heavenly power, you constantly intercede for all humanity. Intercede for us, O Holy Mother of God.

The Feast of the Birth of Mary
(September 8)

Hail Mary! You are full of grace! You are a true daughter of Zion and the joy of your parents. We celebrate your birth which proclaims joy to the whole world. The first rays of our coming salvation would break upon the scene at your birth, signaling the untying of the knot of Eve's disobedience. All creation rejoiced to see your coming. Your life has inspired and illumined the church. Intercede for us, O Holy Mother of God.

The Solemnity of the Immaculate Conception
(December 8)

Hail Mary! You are full of grace! You were chosen before the world began to bear the Son of God. You are the highest honored of our race, Holy Virgin Mary. You were prepared from the moment of conception to be the mother of your Son, to be untouched by the stain of sin. You experienced the perfection of God's saving power. We follow joyfully in your footsteps. Draw us after you in the way of holiness. Intercede for us, O Holy Mother of God.

Litany of the Blessed Virgin Mary
(Litany of Loreto)

Lord, have mercy.	*Lord, have mercy.*
Christ, have mercy.	*Christ, have mercy.*
Christ hear us.	*Christ, graciously hear us.*
God, the Father of heaven,	*have mercy on us.*
God, the Son,	
redeemer of the world,	*have mercy on us.*
God, the Holy Spirit,	*have mercy on us.*
Holy Trinity, one God,	*have mercy on us.*
Holy Mary,	*pray for us.*
Holy Mother of God,	*pray for us.*
Holy Virgin of virgins,	*pray for us.*
Mother of Christ,	*pray for us.*
Mother of divine grace,	*pray for us.*
Mother most pure,	*pray for us.*
Mother most chaste,	*pray for us.*
Mother inviolate,	*pray for us.*
Mother undefiled,	*pray for us.*
Mother most lovable,	*pray for us.*

Mother most admirable,	*pray for us.*
Mother of good counsel,	*pray for us.*
Mother of our creator,	*pray for us.*
Mother of our Savior,	*pray for us.*
Virgin most prudent,	*pray for us.*
Virgin most venerable,	*pray for us.*
Virgin most renowned,	*pray for us.*
Virgin most powerful,	*pray for us.*
Virgin most merciful,	*pray for us.*
Virgin most faithful,	*pray for us.*
Mirror of justice,	*pray for us.*
Seat of wisdom,	*pray for us.*
Cause of our joy,	*pray for us.*
Spiritual vessel,	*pray for us.*
Vessel of honor,	*pray for us.*
Singular vessel of devotion,	*pray for us.*
Mystical rose,	*pray for us.*
Tower of David,	*pray for us.*
Tower of ivory,	*pray for us.*
House of gold,	*pray for us.*
Ark of the covenant,	*pray for us.*
Gate of heaven,	*pray for us.*
Morning star,	*pray for us.*
Health of the sick,	*pray for us.*
Refuge of sinners,	*pray for us.*
Comfort of the afflicted,	*pray for us.*
Help of Christians,	*pray for us.*
Queen of angels,	*pray for us.*
Queen of patriarchs,	*pray for us.*
Queen of prophets,	*pray for us.*

Queen of apostles,	*pray for us.*
Queen of martyrs,	*pray for us.*
Queen of confessors,	*pray for us.*
Queen of virgins,	*pray for us.*
Queen of all saints,	*pray for us.*
Queen conceived without original sin,	*pray for us.*
Queen assumed into heaven,	*pray for us.*
Queen of the most holy rosary,	*pray for us.*
Queen of peace,	*pray for us.*
Lamb of God, you take away the sins of the world,	*spare us, O Lord.*
Lamb of God, you take away the sins of the world,	*graciously, hear us, O Lord.*
Lamb of God, you take away the sins of the world,	*have mercy on us.*

Pray for us, O holy Mother of God.
That we may be made worthy of the promises of Christ.

Let us pray: Grant that we your servants, Lord, may enjoy unfailing health of mind and body, and through the prayers of the ever Blessed Virgin Mary in her glory, free us from our sorrows in this world and give us eternal happiness in the next. Through Christ our Lord. *Amen.*

Selected Bibliography

Angelica, Mother M., *The Promised Woman* (Birmingham, AL: Journey into Scripture, 1977).

Bensman, Mary Lee, *Through Mary's Eyes* (Avon, NJ: Magnificat Press, 1991).

Brookby, Peter ed., *Virgin Wholly Marvelous* (Cambridge, MA: The Ravengate Press, 1981).

Buckley, Msgr. Michael comp., *The Catholic Prayer Book* (Ann Arbor, MI: Servant Books, 1986).

Carroll, Warren H., *Our Lady of Guadalupe and the Conquest of Darkness* (Front Royal, VA: Cristendom Publications, 1983).

Delaney, John J. ed., *A Woman Clothed with the Sun* (New York, NY: Doubleday, 1960).

Doherty, Catherine de Hueck, *Our Lady's Unknown Mysteries* (Combermere, Ontario: Madonna House Publications, 1990).

Dollen, Fr. Charles trans., *A Voice Said Ave!* (Boston, MA: Daughters of St. Paul, 1963).

Fiorelli, Fr. Lewis S., O.S.F.S. ed., *The Sermons of St. Francis de Sales on Our Lady* (Rockford, IL: Tan Books and Publishers, 1985).

Hartman, Charles ed., *The Life of Mary, Mother of Jesus* (New York, NY: Guild Press, 1963).

Hinnebusch, Paul, O.P., *Mother of Jesus Present with Us* (Libertyville, IL: Prow Books, 1980).

Houselander, Caryll, *The Flowering Tree* (Kansas City, MO: Sheed and Ward, 1945).

_____, *Lift Up Your Hearts* (New York, NY: Arena Lettres, 1978).

_____, *The Reed of God* (New York, NY: Arena Lettres, 1944).

Hutchinson, Gloria, *Mary and Inner Healing: An Armchair Pilgrimage to Lourdes* (Cincinnati, OH: St. Anthony Messenger Press, 1980).

Jelly, Frederick M., O.P., *Madonna: Mary in the Catholic Tradition* (Huntington, IN: Our Sunday Visitor, Inc., 1986).

John Paul II, *Mary, God's Yes to Man* (Harrison, NY: Ignatius Press, 1988).

Johnston, Francis, *Fatima: The Great Sign* (Rockford, IL: Tan Books and Publishers, Inc., 1980).

_____, *The Wonder of Guadalupe* (Rockford, IL: Tan Books and Publishers, Inc., 1981).

Liguori, St. Alphonsus de, *The Glories of Mary* (Brooklyn, NY: Redemptorist Fathers, 1931).

Lynch, John W., *A Woman Wrapped in Silence* (Mahwah, NJ: Paulist Press, 1968).

Little, Dr. Joyce A., Ph.D., *The Significance of Mary for Women* (Washington, NJ: World Apostolate of Fatima, 1989).

Maloney, George A., S.J., *Mary: The Womb of God* (Denville, NJ: Dimension Books, 1976).

Montague, George, S.M., *Our Father, Our Mother: Mary and the Faces of God* (Steubenville, OH: Franciscan University Press, 1990).

Montfort, St. Louis de, *The Secret of Mary* (Bay Shore, NY: Montfort Publications, 1962).

_____, *The Secret of the Rosary* (Bay Shore, NY: Montfort Publications, 1954).

_____, *True Devotion to Mary* (Rockford, IL: Tan Books and Publishers, Inc., 1985).

O'Connor, Edward D., C.S.C. ed., *The Mystery of the Woman* (Notre Dame, IN: University of Notre Dame Press, 1956).

Odell, Catherine M., *Those Who Saw Her: The Apparitions of Mary* (Huntington, IN: Our Sunday Visitor Inc., 1986).

O'Donnell, Christopher, O. Carm., *Life in the Spirit and Mary* (Wilmington, DE: Michael Glazier, Inc., 1981).

Paul VI, *Mary—God's Mother and Ours* (Boston, MA: Daughters of St. Paul, 1979).

Pelletier, Joseph A., A.A., *Mary Our Mother* (Worcester, MA: Assumption Publications, 1972).

_____ , *The Sun Danced at Fatima* (New York, NY: Doubleday, 1983).

Pursley, Leo A., D.D., *The Perfect Woman* (Boston, MA: Daughters of St. Paul, 1973).

Rahner, Karl, *Mary, Mother of the Lord* (New York, NY: Herder and Herder, 1963).

Randall, Rev. John, Helen P. Hawkinson, and **Sharyn Malloy**, *Mary: Pathway to Fruitfulness* (Hauppaugh, NY: Living Flame Press, 1978).

Rojas, Carmen, *Draw Me: Catholic Prayers for Every Occasion in a Woman's Life* (Ann Arbor, MI: Servant Publications, 1990).

Rosage, Rev. Msgr. David E., *Mary, the Model Charismatic* (Boston, MA: St. Paul Books and Media, undated).

Roschini, Gabriel M., O.S.M., *The Virgin Mary in the Writings of Maria Valtorta* (Sherbrooke, Quebec: Kolbe's Publications, 1989).

Rotelle, John, O.S.A., ed., *Mary's Yes: Meditations on Mary Through the Ages* (Ann Arbor, MI: Servant Publications, 1988).

Rouville, Alexander de, *Imitation of Mary* (New York, NY: Catholic Book Publishing Co., 1977-1985).

Schillebeeckx, Edward, O.P., *Mary, Mother of the Redemption* (Kansas City, MO: Sheed and Ward, 1964).

Schlink, Basilea, *Mary, the Mother of Jesus* (Germany: Evangelical Sisterhood of Mary, 1986).

Sharkey, Don, *The Woman Shall Conquer* (Libertyville, IL: Prow Books, 1976).

Sheed, F.J., *The Mary Book* (Kansas City, MO: Sheed and Ward, 1950).

Sheen, Fulton J., *The World's First Love* (New York, NY: Doubleday, 1956).

Suenens, Cardinal L.J., *Mary, the Mother of God* (New York, NY: Hawthorne Books, 1959).

Therese, Sister M., ed., *I Sing of a Maiden: The Mary Book of Verse* (New York: NY: Macmillan, 1947).

Walsh, William Thomas, *Our Lady of Fatima* (New York, NY: Macmillan, 1954).

Weiger, Josef, *Mary, Mother of Faith* (Washington, DC: Henry Regnery Co., 1959).

Acknowledgments

The editor and publisher wish to express their gratitude to the following for permission to reprint material of which they are the authors, publishers, and/or copyright holders.

Excerpts from *The Promised Woman* by Mother M. Angelica, © Journey into Scripture 1977. Our Lady of the Angels Monastery, Inc., Birmingham, Alabama 35210. Used by permission.

Prayers from *Through Mary's Eyes*, © 1991 by Mary Lee Bensman, published by Magnificat Press, Avon, New Jersey 07717. Used by permission.

Excerpts from *Our Lady of Guadalupe and the Conquest of Darkness* by Warren H. Carroll, © 1983 by Christendom Educational Corporation, published by Christendom Publications, Front Royal, Virginia 22630. Used by permission.

Excerpts from *The Way* by Josemaria Escriva de Balaguer, © 1979 Scepter Publishers, New Rochelle, New York 10801. Used by permission.

Excerpts from *A Woman Clothed with the Sun*, © 1960 by John J. Delaney; *The Sun Danced at Fatima*, © 1983 by Joseph A. Pelletier, A. A.; *Daily We Touch Him*, © 1977 by M. Basil Pennington, O.C.S.O.; and *The World's First Love*, © 1956 by Fulton J. Sheen. Published by Doubleday, New York, New York 10103. Used by permission.

Excerpts from *The Reign of Jesus Through Mary* by Gabriel Denis, S.M.M., © 1944 by Montfort Publications, and *The Secret of Mary* by St. Louis de Montfort as adapted by Eddie Doherty, © 1962 by Montfort Publications, Bay Shore, New York 11706. Used by permission.

Excerpts from *Our Lady's Unknown Mysteries* by Catherine de Hueck Doherty, © 1990 by Madonna House Publications, Combermere, Ontario, Canada K0J 1L0. Used by permission.

Excerpts from *Our Lady of the Most Blessed Sacrament* by St. Peter

261

Excerpts from *The God of the Impossible*, © 1975 by June Miller, published by Zondervan Publishing House, Grand Rapids, Michigan 49506.

Excerpts from *Day by Day With My Daily Visitor* compiled and edited by Patrick R. Moran, © 1980 by Our Sunday Visitor, Inc., and *Those Who Saw Her: The Apparitions of Mary* by Catherine M. Odell, © 1986 by Our Sunday Visitor, Inc., Huntington, Indiana 46750. Used by permission.

Excerpts from *Vatican II: Marian Council* by William G. Most, © 1972 by St. Paul Publications, Ireland. Used by permission.

"Our Lady of the Refugees" by Sister Maura Eichner, S.S.N.D., used by permission of the author.

Excerpts from *Our Father, Our Mother: Mary and the Faces of God*, © 1990 by George T. Montague, S.M., published by Franciscan University Press, Steubenville, Ohio. Used by permission.

Excerpts by Walter J. Burghardt, S.J., and Ferrer Smith, O.P., from *The Mystery of the Woman* edited by Edward D. O'Connor, C.S.C., © 1956 by University of Notre Dame Press, Notre Dame, Indiana 46556. Used by permission.

Excerpts from *Life in the Spirit and Mary* by Christopher O'Donnell, O.Carm., © 1981 by Michael Glazier, Inc., Wilmington, Delaware 19801.

Excerpts from *Mary—God's Mother and Ours* by Pope Paul VI, © 1979 Daughters of St. Paul; *The Perfect Woman* by Leo A. Pursley, © 1973 by Daughters of St. Paul; *A Voice Said Ave!*, translated by Fr. Charles Dollen, © 1963 Daughters of St. Paul; and *Mary, The Model Charismatic* by David E. Rosage. Published by St. Paul Books and Media (Daughters of St. Paul), Boston, Massachusetts 02130. Used by permission.

Excerpts from *Father Payton's Rosary Prayer Book*, © The Family Rosary, Inc., Albany, New York 12203. Used by permission.

"Mary Was a Meadow" from the cassette *Mary Songs/More Mary Songs* by Bill Peffley, © 1985 Balance House Publications, 201 E. Main St., Norristown, PA 19401. Used by permission.

Excerpts from *Mary Our Mother*, © 1972 by Joseph A. Pelletier, A.A., published by Assumption Publications, Worcester, Massachusetts 01609. Used by permission.

Excerpts from *Prayers* by Michel Quoist, © 1963 by Sheed & Ward, Inc., and *Mary, Mother of the Redemption* by Edward Schillebeeckx, © 1964 by Sheed & Ward, Inc., Kansas City, Missouri 64141-6492. Used by permission.

Excerpts from *Mary, Mother of the Lord*, © 1963 by Karl Rahner,